USING COMPUTERS

Jerome M. Clubb
Michael W. Traugott

Center for Political Studies
and Inter-University Consortium
for Political and Social Research
The University of Michigan

A Publication of
The Division of Educational Affairs
of the
American Political Science Association
1527 New Hampshire Ave. N.W.
Washington, D.C. 20036

USING COMPUTERS

by

Jerome M. Clubb
Michael W. Traugott

Center for Political Studies
and
Inter-University Consortium for Political and Social Research
The University of Michigan

Division of Educational Affairs
The American Political Science Association
1527 New Hampshire Avenue, N.W.
Washington, D.C. 20036

The preparation of *Using Computers* was supported by Grant GY 9351 from the National Science Foundation to the American Political Science Association for a project to improve undergraduate education in political science. Sheilah R. Koeppen, Director of the Division of Educational Affairs, is the project director. Responsibility to the profession for the project activities, 1972-1975, is exercised by this Steering Committee on Undergraduate Education:

> Vernon Van Duke, Chairman, University of Iowa
> Vincent J. Browne, Jr., Howard University
> Gloria Carrig, Loop College, City Colleges of Chicago
> Heinz Eulau, Stanford University
> Betty Nesvold, California State University, San Diego
> Jack Peltason, Chancellor, University of Illinois
> Ithiel de S. Pool, Massachusetts Institute of Technology
> James A. Robinson, President, University of West Florida
> Stanley Rothman, Smith College

This monograph has been commissioned by the Steering Committee on Undergraduate Education. It has been reviewed by three qualified persons, including a member of the Steering Committee. The monograph is published under the auspices of the Division of Educational Affairs. However, the views expressed are those of the contributors and not of the Steering Committee of the American Political Science Association.

Table of Contents

Introduction

For many of us computers are mysterious and even intimidating devices. For some the term may conjure up little more than images of banks of blinking lights perhaps on the bridge of the starship *Enterprise*. For others the image may be more malicious—a pernicious device that debits accounts but never credits them; that commits errors but rejects corrections; that routes objects to mistaken destinations; and which, through misguided efforts to gain efficiency and reduce expenditures of human energy and time, hopelessly confuses processes and procedures by rendering the simple complex.

In fact, computational equipment is mysterious, but only in the sense that the internal combustion engine is mysterious to those without mechanical expertise, training or interest. Although an automobile can be used effectively even in total ignorance of the internal mechanical intricacies of the engine, at least limited and superficial knowledge of these matters often proves useful for even the occasional driver if only to allow sensible and wary intercourse with service station attendants, mechanics, and automobile dealers. Much the same can be said of the use of computational equipment. That equipment can be used effectively, meaningfully, and even innovatively by those without knowledge beyond the simple information analogous to that required to drive an automobile. Here again, however, at least limited additional knowledge is useful if only in order to recognize the potentialities of computational equipment, to avoid intimidation, and to deal meaningfully and warily with those who are knowledgeable and upon whom dependence must be placed for expert advice and guidance.

This is not to say that computational equipment is simple. Indeed, even the smallest item of computational equipment is a monument to scientific and engineering genius. On the other hand, computers can perform no tasks that human beings cannot, and in fact they perform only a few relatively simple operations: essentially arithmetic operations, logical comparisons, and listing. It is only that they can perform these operations in virtually infinite sequences and combinations, at very high speed, and with almost total accuracy. Thus computers are immensely valuable for the control and ordering of information, for the performance of extensive and repetitive calculation, and for the control, regulation and simulation of complex processes; and their use makes large and complicated tasks possible which would be impractical if only human energy were available. It is for these reasons that computational equipment is an invaluable tool for research and instructional use in the social sciences and that it has facilitated new approaches to research and instruction and brought about new research findings and the advancement of new instructional goals.

These perspectives constitute the basis for the present monograph. Those who seek a detailed discussion of transistors, microcircuitry, electronic architecture and the like will be disappointed by what follows. Such matters are of no interest to many, of passing interest to some, of avocational interest to a few, and of both avocational and vocational interest to a still smaller number. This is not to celebrate ignorance. It is rather that knowledge of such matters is not a requisite for meaningful and effective research and instructional applications of computational equipment. On the other hand, even the very limited and essentially unsophisticated references to technical issues that appear below may seem excessive to some. We have only attempted to provide in essentially non-technical terms that information required to aid those without prior training and experience who wish to begin to apply computational equipment in their research and instruction.

In what follows, the reader will encounter a variety of terms that may appear to be no more than jargon. Computational equipment reflects new scientific and technological developments, new applications of scientific principles, new processes, and a new range of human activities. Inevitably and necessarily new words and terms have been devised to describe these machines and their operation. In any event, whether jargon or not, these new words and terms, and new uses of old words and terms, are an intrinsic part of the computational world. Part of the process of "demystifying" computational equipment and learning to use that equipment in the service of meaningful instructional and research goals is to come to grips with what may seem to the inexperienced an arcane and alien terminology. A glossary is appended which contains definitions of most of the technical terms used in the text.

We have attempted to avoid one particular type of terminology. In our view, a distressing aspect of computer technology has been the tendency to anthropomorphize computing and computational equipment. Computers are referred to as "reading" and "writing," as "thinking" and "expecting"; and numerous other anthropomorphic terms are used to refer to and describe electromechanical processes. But computers *are* no more than electromechanical devices, and terminological attribution to them of human properties can only serve to confuse and to increase the misguided awe in which they are sometimes held. Yet such terms are widely used, and no other terms have been devised to refer to various computational processes. Although we have attempted to minimize and avoid the use of anthropomorphic terms, that effort has been less than successful.

Because of their very mechanical nature, computers cannot judge what the analyst "really" meant. The successful use of the computer in a specific application depends directly on the quality of instructions which the user supplies. There is need for meticulous accuracy, attention to detail, and specificity. As a result, the reader will find a great deal of stress placed upon accuracy in what follows. One of the most difficult—and disconcerting—adjustments that the beginner has to make in learning to work with computers is to the rigidity of specification that is required for their successful use. Because of the very high levels of abstraction at which they operate, the exact specification of the instructions required for a specific application leaves no room for deviation. Many novice users must endure an extended period of adjustment to "errors" as they learn that synonyms or variations in spelling are not the equivalent of the necessary instructions. It is similarly the case that an expression beginning in column ten of a punched card, for example, has no necessary or meaningful relationship to the exact same expression beginning in column eleven. These basic elements involved in data preparation and submission of computer jobs are simple, but the user must follow them exactly for success. This is, of course, simply a manifestation of the fact that computers do not think for themselves but are operated on the basis of fixed and rigid electronic and mechanical principles.

The organization of the monograph is simple and straightforward. An initial chapter details the components of computational systems, including the principal physical devices and the languages used to write operating instructions. The second chapter is concerned with the principles of data collection and introduces the reader to the concepts associated with datasets and their characteristics. These discussions are extended to the detailed elements of data preparation in the third chapter, including the design of formats, coding schemes, and documentation. In the following chapter, the transcription of information to computer-readable form and preliminary data processing are reviewed. Chapter Five contains a discussion of applications software, including a comparison of the major social science software packages currently available and which the reader is likely to encounter. The sixth chapter is concerned with the instructional uses of computers and incorporates a review of several alternative applications. The treatment in this chapter is brief and directed primarily toward data-based applications. There is a limited discussion devoted to simulations and various types of computer aided instruction techniques. While we consider these applications to be important and of increasing significance to political scientists, there are other monographs in this series which contain extensive and detailed descriptions of relevant computer-based instructional techniques. Where appropriate the reader is referred to other sources for more extended treatment. The final chapter presents a summary of the authors' views of the major trends in social science computing and of the ways in which they are likely to affect applications in political science.

We are grateful to our associates Gregory A. Marks and John E. Stuckey who read various portions of the original manuscript and suggested revisions. We are especially indebted to three anonymous reviewers who provided us with valuable suggestions for additions and revisions to the text. For any errors or misstatements which occur, we alone remain responsible.

CHAPTER I.
Computational Systems

Those who employ computers for research, teaching, or other purposes must rely upon what we will call *computational systems.* The term system is appropriate whatever the magnitude or scope of the particular application and whether or not the user is aware of all of the elements of the system employed. (In the jargon of the area, those who employ computers for particular applications are often referred to as *users.*) For present purposes, computational systems can usefully be seen as composed of three basic elements: a set of electronic and mechanical devices, often called *hardware;* a set of computer programs, often called *software,* which direct these devices in the performance of particular tasks in specified ways; and, finally, a supporting administrative structure. The latter element is composed of individuals in varying numbers who manage the system and provide assistance in its use, and a series of more or less formal administrative rules of varying complexity which govern the use of the system.

It is probably common to think of the *computer* as no more than a particular configuration of equipment or, perhaps, as only a single item of equipment. Viewed in these terms, the nature and magnitude of the computational tasks that can be carried out are probably seen as entirely a function of the size and complexity of the available equipment. It is more useful, however, to think of computer applications in broader systemic terms. As will be seen, the kinds of applications that can be carried out using a particular system, and the ease and efficiency with which those applications can be executed, are governed and limited not only by the nature of the hardware component of the system but also by the nature of the available software, by the characteristics of the administrative and supporting structure, and by the combination of those elements.

Computer Hardware

Configurations of computing equipment vary widely from one computer installation (center) to the next. In the most general terms, however, it is possible to speak of four different categories of computational functions and associated devices: input, processing, storage and output. The meaning of these terms is at least conceptually self-evident. Input devices are used to introduce information, including both research or instructional data and programs; processing devices, usually referred to as *central processing units (CPU),* perform the actual manipulation of information; storage devices are used to retain information; and output devices reproduce information, usually the results of the particular processing work, either in "humanly-readable" form for visual examination or in "machine-readable" form suitable for subsequent further processing.

These various functions can be given more concrete illustration by imagining a hypothetical analysis to be carried out using a simple, and also hypothetical, hardware configuration. Such a configuration and its functions are depicted in Figure I-1. In terms of such a configuration, information consisting of both the computer program and the data to be subjected to a particular analysis procedure are recorded on the standard 80-column punch cards. The information recorded on cards is introduced ("read") into the system using a *card reader* and then routed either directly to the central processing unit or intermediately stored on a storage device, such as a *magnetic tape* or *disk,* and subsequently routed to the central processing unit. The central processing unit is used to carry out the arithmetic, mathematical or other manipulations involved in the analysis task as instructed by the program. The results of the specified manipulations are then printed ("output") using a line printer, or held temporarily on a storage device to be printed subsequently. A copy of the original data might be maintained on tape or disk for subsequent further processing or simply erased ("scratched") and removed from the system. In the latter case, the cards recording the original data could be retained for further use.

This illustration is of course oversimplified. On the other hand, the equipment and functions depicted in Figure I-1 are by no means completely at odds with the actual characteristics of many hardware configurations. Obviously, however, there is much more to the story. Even the simplest hardware configuration includes a variety of control and other ancillary devices which are omitted from consideration here. A variety of devices are used to perform the functions depicted in Figure I-1, and several individual devices perform more than one of these functions. In other words, input devices also serve as output devices and storage devices also serve at times as both output and input devices.

A variety of devices are available to input information which utilize keyboard terminals. Other input devices, although not widely available, include the *paper tape reader* and *optical character reader* (OCR), which are used to interpret (read) particular type fonts or character sets or information recorded with special markings and translate them into machine-readable form. Output devices, in addition to line printers and keyboard terminals, include terminals with cathode ray tubes (CRT's similar to television tubes) which display information in humanly-readable form, card punch machines which output information in the form of punched cards, devices which output information in the form of either microfilm or microfiche, and a variety of other output devices are also used.

The most commonly used storage devices are magnetic tapes and disks, although numerous other devices, which will not be discussed here, are also employed for this purpose. And as was suggested above, information is not only stored on such devices but is also input from these devices for processing and output to these devices when processing is completed. Only a little thought will make clear, moreover, that information processing is not confined to the central processing unit. Thus, while the meaning of the terms input, output, storage and processing may be conceptually clear, it is probably best to think of these terms not in reference to specific devices but as functions which are performed in various ways by various devices.

Input, output and storage devices are frequently referred to as *peripherals* or peripheral devices. Examples of these are referred to in Figure I-2. The central processing unit can probably appropriately be seen as the heart of computer hardware configurations. It is here that arithmetic and mathematical calculations are carried out, that processes are simulated, information managed, and the other hardware elements of the configuration controlled. The central processing unit can usefully be seen in conceptual terms as comprised of three components. The *monitor* or *executive system* contains the primary set of operating instructions for the equipment. It defines the operating power or capabilities of the system

FIGURE I-1

**Functions and Equipment of a
Hypothetical Computer Hardware Configuration**

(Dotted lines indicate alternative routes.)

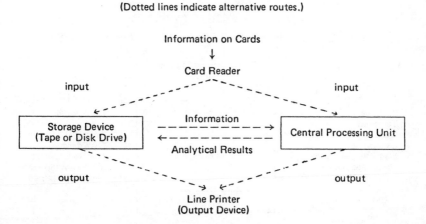

in terms of the number and complexity of the instructions that can be employed, the speed at which they can be carried out, and the magnitude of information that can be managed. A second element is the *arithmetic unit* which contains instructions for performing basic arithmetic operations. Although it is quite common to think of computers as giant calculators, they are in fact capable of a wide range of more general symbolic manipulations. Because computers are often used to perform large numbers of repetitive arithmetic calculations, however, a special area in the central processing unit is devoted to these operating functions. The third working area of the central processing unit is the *memory unit*. This is the location where data are stored and operated upon during processing using data in the most general sense to include both software (programs) as well as specific items of information.

Each storage location in memory can be identified by an *address*, providing the means for locating and manipulating the information. The memory unit in the central processing unit is often referred to as *real* or *core memory*. In complex computing configurations, certain peripheral devices are used for storage as a system of *virtual memory* which is immediately accessible to the central processing unit and which, from the standpoint of the user, is indistinguishable from core memory. In this way the capacity of the central processing unit can be greatly increased.

In a basic sense, all computer hardware works to record, interpret, store or manipulate information through a simple "yes-no" or "on-off" principle which involves the passage of electrical current (on) or its impedance (off). The operation of this simple principle can perhaps be most easily conceptualized by considering the standard 80-column punch card. Information is recorded on such cards by punching holes in a fixed matrix format consisting of columns and rows. A hole (or holes) punched in a given row (or rows) of a particular column records a particular number, letter or other character in that column. By punching holes in

FIGURE I-2

The Conceptual Elements of a Computer Hardware Installation

Central Processing Unit (CPU)

Input Devices		Central Processing Unit (CPU)		Output Devices
Card reader		Monitor (Executive) System		Card punch
Terminal				Line printer
Optical scanner	→		→	Terminal
Disk drive				Disk drive
Magnetic tape drive		Memory Unit		Magnetic tape drive
Paper tape reader				Microfilm tape drive
				Paper tape punch
		Arithmetic Unit		

particular rows of contiguous columns, larger numbers or names composed of more than one character can be recorded. The numbers or letters so recorded may be real arithmetic values, such as the vote cast in a particular district, or actual alphabetic names, or they may be coded values which are used to represent particular concepts, facts or measures. In either case, of course, recording information by punching holes in cards involves encoding that information according to agreed upon conventions which are standardized but otherwise arbitrary.

Information recorded on punched cards is introduced (read) into the CPU by means of another element of the hardware configuration called a *card reader*. Using the reader, the cards are passed between a bank of metallic brushes and a bank of contact points which correspond to the columns of the cards. When the card enters, the flow of electrical current between the brushes and the contact points is interrupted (off). When a hole is encountered in a particular column and row, contact between a particular brush and its associated point is made. Current flows (on) and a signal is produced which indicates the presence of a particular character in a particular location. That signal is transmitted to a storage area of the hardware and the character is recorded on that device. Of course, this process occurs at a very high rate of speed. In the space of time required to read this paragraph, several hundred punched cards could have been read by a card reader.

In order to understand the way in which information is recorded on other devices, additional complications must be considered. It is necessary to consider these matters, however, in order to understand references to the capacities of computational devices and to be better able to conceptualize their operation. From the representation of information by punched holes in cards, the data are translated into bits as an electromagnetic form. A *bit* is the smallest unit of data, represented by a 0 or 1 without the usual numeric significance. Groups of these bits are usually operated on as an entity called a *byte* or sometimes as a *word* of a fixed number of bytes.

Information is presented in Figure I-3 to illustrate three alternative representations of the standard numeric digits and alphabetic characters. The three entries in the figure include, in the first column, the common printed representations of the characters, followed by the equivalent representation on a standard punch card by one or more holes in a single card column, and finally the electromagnetic representation of the same information in a standard eight-bit binary code which is in wide use. For example, the number "1" is represented on a punched card by a hole in the "1" row for a given column. As described above, electricity is conducted between a brush and a metal surface as the hole in the card passes between them, and the impulse is translated into a storage area of the computer as a representation of the number.

In the case of the electromagnetic eight-bit code, a binary system of eight impulses is used to represent the number. In each of the locations, a bit of information is recorded as an electronic impulse on a magnetic surface as either "on" (indicated by a 1) or "off" (indicated by a 0). The eight bits are divided into two four-bit segments. In the second segment, as illustrated in Figure I-3, the numbers are represented as the sum of the arithmetic powers of 2, with an "on" impulse in a given position indicating which values contribute to the sum. For the representation of numbers, the first four-bit segment contains all "on" impulses. In our example, then,

FIGURE I-3
Three Alternative Forms of Data Representation

Common Printed Character	is the equivalent of	Representation in Single Column Punched Card Code	is the equivalent of	Representation in Electromagnetic 8-Bit Code
0		0		1111 0000
1		1		1111 0001
2		2		1111 0010
3		3		1111 0011
4		4		1111 0100
5		5		1111 0101
6		6		1111 0110
7		7		1111 0111
8		8		1111 1000
9		9		1111 1001
A		12-1		1100 0001
B		12-2		1100 0010
C		12-3		1100 0011
D		12-4		1100 0100
E		12-5		1100 0101
F		12-6		1100 0110
G		12-7		1100 0111
H		12-8		1100 1000
I		12-9		1100 1001
J		11-1		1101 0001
K		11-2		1101 0010
L		11-3		1101 0011
M		11-4		1101 0100
N		11-5		1101 0101
O		11-6		1101 0110
P		11-7		1101 0111
Q		11-8		1101 1000
R		11-9		1101 1001
S		0-2		1110 0010
T		0-3		1110 0011
U		0-4		1110 0100
V		0-5		1110 0101
W		0-6		1110 0110
X		0-7		1110 0111
Y		0-8		1110 1000
Z		0-9		1110 1001

the number "1" is represented in standard eight-bit code as 1111 0001, and the number "2" as 1111 0010.

It is important to note the importance of having an agreed upon set of conventions for data representation. The very magnitude of the combinations and permutations of alternative coding schemes is so great that the transfer of information between individuals or institutions would be almost impossible unless these standards were in place. In a card-image computing environment it is worth emphasizing that it is only the appearance of a standard code in a standard size card, also an agreed upon convention, that is of any significance in computing. The color of the card or any printed pictures on the face have no effect whatsoever on the interpretation of the encoded information by the computer.

When we talk about the quantity of this kind of coded information which can be stored in a computer's memory, the usual scale is 1,000's of *bytes*, the smallest unit of information which can be read by a single program instruction. The notation *"K"* is used by convention to denote 1,024 bytes (2^{10} bytes); therefore a "128K" machine is a computer with a memory capacity of 131,072 bytes of information. Large quantities of data, defined here as information stored on several thousands of punched cards, are rarely stored in the main memory of the computer but rather on such devices as magnetic tapes or disks. Each of these devices provides considerable off-line storage of data in two distinct forms of accessibility.

Data are stored on magnetic tapes in a sequential fashion in byte notation. That is to say, the medium operates just as an audio tape. There is a clear beginning of the tape and then one piece of information (the electrical signal) follows another in a sequential fashion for the length of the tape. The standard length of a magnetic tape is 2400 feet. Information can be recorded according to a range of densities, the most common of which are 800 or 1600 bits per inch (BPI or sometimes characters per inch—CPI), although the most current *tape drives* (the devices on which magnetic tapes are mounted for use) record at multiple densities as high as 6250 BPI. If information were written on the entire surface length of a magnetic tape at the highest density, the data stored in this form would be the equivalent of approximately 2.25 million punched cards.

In the preceding pages, three types of information storage devices— punched cards, magnetic tape and disk—were considered and certain of their properties discussed. We will return in a later chapter to discuss the operation of these devices in detail. A rather wide variety of other storage devices are also employed including data cells and data drums. The latter two pieces of hardware, along with other *mass storage devices*, are in virtually all cases a part of the hardware system and seldom encountered directly by the user. Hence they can be omitted from consideration here. Indeed, disks are also usually part of the hardware system and not often directly encountered. In what follows, however, a brief further discussion will be devoted to this form of data storage device in order to describe additional characteristics of computational systems.

Punch cards are probably the most familiar form of information storage for computer applications. Not only do punch cards have the advantage of familiarity, but information stored on punch cards is also, at least in some sense of the word, more tangible than is information stored as magnetic signals on tape or disk. Information stored on cards is also more susceptible to direct examination than is information stored on tape or disk, especially when the interpretation of the punches is printed over each column at the top of the card. Thus the beginning user may feel more comfortable with cards as a storage medium. Moreover, cards are relatively cheap, transportable, and, as will be seen, cards are a kind of "lowest common denominator" that can be used on virtually any computational system. On the other hand, cards are bulky, require substantial space to store, deteriorate easily under adverse temperature and humidity conditions and extended use, and lack the flexibility of other storage forms. Thus, although very widely used for the initial tasks of recording information, the use of cards for long-term information storage or for other aspects of computer processing is becoming less common.

As the preceding comments have suggested, magnetic tape has numerous advantages over cards as a storage medium. Information can be stored much more compactly on tape than on cards, and tape, if properly cared for, is also a highly durable medium. In terms of capacity, moreover, tape is substantially cheaper than cards. Data for more than one research or instructional application can be stored on tape in the form of high density electromagnetic signals is much greater as well.

Both punch cards and magnetic tapes are used to store information in a sequential manner. That is to say, the first card must be read before the second, and so on, just as the first item of information recorded on a tape must be read before the second. A magnetic disk stores data in three dimensions, and an item of information can be accessed directly on the disk as opposed to sequentially. Disks resemble stacks of phonograph records fixed at equal intervals on a hollow spindle. A *disk drive* (the device on which disks are mounted for use) includes a series of arms which move across the surfaces of the disk interpreting the electromagnetic signals which record information. Each surface of the disk is composed of concentric circles with storage locations called tracks; the tracks conceptually form cylinders through the surfaces. The arms of the disk drive can be directed by a control unit on the disk drive to any location for an item of information without having to read all of the information in the prior locations. The arms can also operate forward and backward, unlike the card reader and tape drives, adding another dimension of flexibility. Disks are also capable of storing considerable amounts of information, even more than magnetic tapes. Because access to information stored on disk by the central processing unit is quick and direct, this device is a common component of hardware systems.

The preceding discussion of information storage devices and media allows a further distinction which is in some degree independent of the specific equipment involved. Information is frequently referred to as stored *off line* or *on line* and information processing is said to occur off line or on line. In the former case, the information in question is stored on a magnetic tape, a dismounted disk, or even cards, external to the system. Human intervention is required to mount the tape, install the disk or read the cards before processing can begin. In the case of on-line storage, information is stored on a device—usually a disk or a data cell or drum—that is immediately accessible to the central processing unit and processing can occur without human intervention by simply addressing a command to the central processing unit. The advantages in terms of convenience of on-line, as opposed to off-line, storage and processing are obvious, and on-line processing capabilities are a requirement of complex computing systems in which many users have immediate access to the central processing unit. As will be suggested, however, significant cost differentials are often involved in the choice between the two approaches.

Computer Software

A second major element of computational systems, as noted above, is computer software. As defined elsewhere, computer software refers to the electronic and non-mechanical sets of instructions that direct computational equipment in the execution of particular tasks. This definition—as in the case of most of the definitions employed here—is by no means precise. It will serve, however, for working purposes. The kinds of computing work that can be performed, the ease and facility with which that work can be carried out, and the manner in which it can be performed are governed not only by the nature of the computational hardware employed but also by the nature of the available software. In practice, the individual that can program—write software—can overcome some of the limitations imposed by the particular configuration of software and hardware available at a given computational installation. The increased flexibility gained through acquisition of programming skill, as will be suggested, is by no means unlimited.

Computer software can be usefully divided into two categories— *applications* and *system* software—although here again the distinction is by no means precise and serves only for working purposes. As the term suggests, applications software refers to programs designed and written to carry out particular information management and analysis tasks. Application programs may be *special purpose* in nature—written to allow execution of a specific task, idiosyncratic to the particular information to be managed or analyzed, written to conform to the requirements of a particular installation, and not readily transferrable to other installations. *General purpose* programs, again as the term implies, are more generalized in nature, written to perform a category of tasks, not limited to particular configurations of information, and in some degree transportable from one installation to another. But whether general or special purpose in nature, applications programs direct the computational system in the performance of single information management and analysis tasks involved in the manipulation of data for research, instructional or other applications. System software can best be seen as, in a sense, an integral part of the computational system. These are general programs which govern the actual operation of the hardware. Thus, the monitor and operating or executive system, in effect, direct the scheduling of tasks, govern the interrelation between hardware elements, direct the flow of tasks from one hardware element to another and, in general, regulate the way in which the hardware can be employed. *Compilers* also can be usefully seen as a component of system software. In effect, compilers are translation capabilities which convert computer programs written in a given form *(program language)* into another form *(machine language)* that can be employed by the central processing unit. As a general rule, those who employ computational systems for application purposes, such as research or instruction, do not work directly with the system software. However, applications programs must be written to conform to the requirements of the system software. Moreover, and as is discussed in a subsequent chapter, packages of powerful, complex, and flexible general purpose information management and analysis programs are available and can be employed at diverse computer installations. Such packages are designed and written to conform to the requirements of particular system software. Whether or not a given package can be implemented at a particular installation depends upon the nature of the system software employed at that installation as well as the nature and capacity of the hardware itself.

Something of the nature of computer software can be understood by considering a relatively simple application. At the heart of any computer program is an *algorithm*, the specific sequence of operations through which information must be passed in the execution of a given task. In generalized form, the algorithm involves a series of conditional "if ... then" operations based upon certain characteristics of the information itself or of the types of operations to be performed. Sections of the algorithm relating to subtasks are called *subroutines*, and to the extent they are conditional in the sense described above, they are employed automatically and as necessary when the specified conditions are met. In addition to analytical subroutines, programs also include *input/output (I/O)* subroutines for reading information in and out of the machine and for formatting and printing the results of the specified operations.

These operations are illustrated by Figure I-4 which provides a flowchart of a task to compute the average salary of individuals in five-year age groups. The flowchart is a diagram of the order of operations to be performed, the conditional operations, and should account for all of the possible contingencies which might arise in the information processing task. The input data for the problem consists of a deck of punched cards containing an individual's age in columns 1 to 3 and the person's income to the nearest cent in columns 7 to 13.

FIGURE I-4.

Flowchart of Program to Compute Average Salaries for Specified Age Intervals

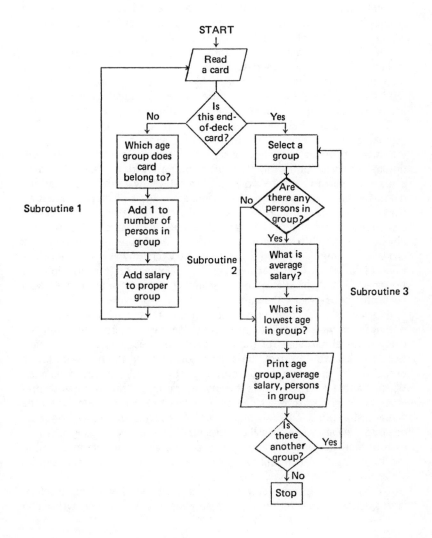

The flowchart indicates that the first step in the process is to read a punched card and ascertain whether it contains relevant information (data) or designates the end of the information file (Subroutine 1). If it is a data card, then the program control passes to a subroutine by which the age field is read first to ascertain to which group the individual belongs. As a result the count of the number of members of that group is incremented by one, and the salary for the individual is added to the total for the group. When all the data have been read and an end-of-job card is encountered, control of the program is transferred to a second subroutine which performs the actual calculations. On a group-by-group basis, a check is made to determine if any data satisfied the appropriate age criterion and then the average salary is computed for the group (Subroutine 2). The results are printed in a specified format until the calculations have been performed for all groups (Subroutine 3), and then the program stops.

This flowchart then describes the entire process from start to finish, beginning and ending with input/output operations and including the statistical manipulations in between. The program contains three conditional loops defining the flow of operations and the subroutines to actually be performed. The flowchart indicates how a card is read and the data assigned to a category, what happens to the collected information when all of the cards have been read, and how the results of the computations are output. The actual problem illustrated in Figure I-4 is obviously a straightforward one. Neither the input/output process nor the analysis is complicated. Other applications would involve operationalizations of algorithms of much greater complexity. But the principles of flowcharting and the use of conditional operations and subroutines would conceptually be exactly the same.

The next step in the process would involve the coding of the algorithm outlined in the flowchart into some language interpretable by the computational hardware for translation into the specific electromechanical signals which would direct the system software and the hardware in the execution of the intended operations in the specific intended manner. When computer programmers specify operating instructions (write programs or program), several languages may be employed to write *(code)* the actual instructions. These include *machine languages, assembler languages, compiler languages* and special-purpose problem oriented languages. Within each of these languages various options are available which are more or less specific to particular machines or which have other special characteristics which might affect their selection.[1]

At the very lowest level of human-machine interaction, machine languages are used. In these languages, instructions can be written in

---

[1] A basic introduction to the derivations and uses of programming languages can be found in Jean E. Sammet, *Programming Languages: History and Fundamentals,* Englewood Cliffs, N.J.: Prentice-Hall, Inc., 1969.

essentially numeric form which are directly interpretable by computer hardware. At present, however, applications programs are rarely written in such languages. There are too many conventions to learn, the language bears little resemblance to normal language, and the complexity of modern hardware and system software and their applications demand instruction sequences of great length. Assembler languages provide one higher level of abstraction for writing computational instructions. Some symbolic notations are utilized for frequently used instructions, but the fundamental need for one assembler language instruction for the comparable machine language instruction remains.

Almost all contemporary applications programming is done in the general purpose symbolic terms made possible through the use of compiler languages. In using compiler languages, the programmer can write instructions in a form more closely resembling the structure of everyday usage, allowing for the special statistical operations often employed and the jargon of computer technicians. The compiler is a program which itself acts as the translater from this form of instruction to basic machine language. The instructions are punched on cards or otherwise entered in the computer in this form *(source code)*, and the result of the compilation is a set of machine language instructions *(object code)* which is generally uninterpretable by most users.

A variety of compiler languages are available, all of which have the general properties outlined above but each of which is suited to particular types of applications. In the social sciences perhaps the most commonly used compiler language is FORTRAN, originally the IBM Formula Translating System developed for mathematical and scientific applications. Although now available in various versions, FORTRAN is a highly generalized and standardized language which, like various other compiler languages, can be employed on numerous types of computers produced by diverse manufacturers. In contrast, machine languages are specific to particular categories and brands of equipment. Hence FORTRAN compilers—as is true of compilers for other generalized languages—are specifically designed for particular types or brands of hardware and are suited to the internal structure and characteristics of each type or brand of machine. There are at present, for example, over 50 different types of FORTRAN compilers in use.

Figure I-5 presents the FORTRAN coded instructions for the application described by the flowchart given in Figure I-4. The entire program is recorded on 18 punch cards. It begins with a card which records only the simple label designated by "C," serving no other function than to identify the program with a comment card. The next card is a format card which describes the location of the input and output data, which is followed by a card recording an instruction to establish two areas *(arrays)* of 20 entries each in core memory to store information on individuals and their salaries. The next three instructions set the initial value in each array element at zero. The next card (statement 1) is the beginning of Subroutine 1, the task which involves the actual reading of data. This first subroutine (or loop) ends at statement number 106, with control being managed by statement 103. Statement 4 begins Subroutine 2 to perform the statistical calculations after the data have been assembled. Statement 7 is the printing step, formatted according to statement 3. The function of the last card is obvious.

Again, FORTRAN is probably the most common and popular compiler language for social scientific applications. Various other compiler languages are also used including COBOL (Common Business Oriented Language), PL/1 (Programming Language 1), and SNOBOL (which is not an acronym). Each of these languages has features and characteristics that make it particularly suitable for specific types of application. In addition to languages such as these, there are also a number of more specialized problem-oriented languages. These include BASIC (Beginner's All-purpose Symbolic Instruction Code), and ALGOL (Algorithm Language). These languages, designed for particular applications, are generally less flexible and powerful, and cannot be used to carry out as wide a variety of tasks as such languages as FORTRAN, COBOL, PL/1 or SNOBOL. On the other hand, these languages more closely resemble conversational language and can be easily used by individuals with specialized substantive skills but limited knowledge of programming languages. In such languages, for example, the verb "ADD" may be used instead of the equivalent symbol "+" as would be required if FORTRAN were used and even higher order instructions, such as "CORRELATE," are sometimes used. Hence these specialized problem-oriented languages are used by some to develop software for particular limited research applications and are often used for instructional purposes with beginning students as well.

We have touched here on only some of the computational languages that are currently available and in use, and we have described computational languages in only the most cursory terms. It should be clear that whether or not a given language can be used at a particular installation depends on the availability of an appropriate compiler, one of the elements of systems software. It is no longer the case that the individual must be familiar with computational languages and skilled in computer programming in order to meaningfully use computational systems for research and instructional purposes. A number of powerful computer program packages are available and can be employed at diverse installations. Indeed, using such packages, some of which are described in a subsequent chapter, advanced and even innovative instructional and research use can be made of computational systems. Whether a particular program package can be used at an installation depends, of course, upon the availability of appropriate compilers, the nature of other elements of systems software, and the nature and capacity of the computational equipment employed at that installation.

FIGURE I-5.

Coded Instructions for the FORTRAN Program to Perform the Operations in the Flowchart in Figure I-4

C FOR COMMENT	STATEMENT NUMBER	FORTRAN STATEMENT
C		POPULATION AND SALARY PROBLEM
	3	FORMAT(I3,F10.12,F7.0)
	100	DIMENSION P(20),S(20)
	101	DO 9 N=1,20
	102	P(N)=0.0
	9	S(N)=0.0
	1	READ 3,K,SAL
	103	IF(K+1)8,4,2
	2	N=K/5+1
	104	P(N)=P(N)+1.0
	105	S(N)=S(N)+SAL
	106	GO TO 1
	4	DO 7 N=1,20
	107	IF(P(N))8,6,5
	5	S(N)=S(N)/P(N)
	6	K=5*N-5
	7	PRINT 3,K,S(N),P(N)
	8	STOP

Administrative Support

Hardware and software are relatively obvious elements of computational systems, and it follows directly that the characteristics of hardware and software effect the ways in which such systems can be used. There is a third element of computational systems which has a significant effect on patterns of use despite the fact that it is in some ways less tangible and more diffuse, less easy to describe in general terms, and certainly varies as widely from one installation to the other as does hardware. This is the administrative support for the system. We can begin, however, with a trite observation: computing installations cost money, and monetary resources are always in too short supply. Thus, decisions must be made as to what hardware and software is to be acquired, implemented and developed, how that hardware and software is to be used, and what supporting facilities are to be provided.

It requires little thought to recognize that initial decisions as to the size and capacity of the hardware to be rented or purchased effect the kinds of computing tasks that can be carried out and the ease with which they can be performed. Similarly, in acquiring hardware, it might be decided to emphasize a powerful central processing unit while, in relative terms, neglecting storage and peripheral devices. Such a decision would be disproportionately advantageous for mathematical and scientific applications and disadvantageous for social science applications since the latter tend to require more in the way of storage and input/output capacity and less in the way of calculational capacity.

Decisions can also be made to concentrate resources on the acquisition of powerful hardware while neglecting software acquisition and development. In such a case, the variety of available compilers is limited as is the range of computing languages that can be employed. Other elements of systems software may limit applications, and the range of applications software is also limited. Moreover, the decision to acquire systems software, such as compilers or an applications program package, is not enough. Software can be made available in a manner that facilitates ease of use or in a manner that makes use difficult, and to remain operational, software requires continued attention *(maintenance)* by skilled personnel. The manner of implementation and the attention given to maintenance restricts or extends utility for applications purposes.

Supporting facilities include equipment such as computer terminals and keypunch machines, manuals and other instructional materials, and personnel. Obviously, effective use of the computational equipment and software depends upon the availability of adequate supporting equipment and instructional material. If only a few terminals and keypunch machines are available, then use of the system is made difficult through scarcity. The number of individuals that can use the system is reduced, and the range of applications limited.

Virtually everyone who employs computers requires at least some assistance in their use. Beginners and students, of course, stand in particular need of advice and assistance. If students encounter difficulty, because of lack of assistance in carrying out computer-based exercises, enthusiasm and interest are likely to wane and instructional goals can be frustrated. Computing installations vary widely in terms of both the quantity and quality of assistance provided to users. At some installations, highly skilled assistance is provided from trained professionals, including assistance in preparing data, submitting work, selecting programs and, in some cases, applications programs are even written to meet the specialized needs of individual users. In such cases, the user needs little in the way of personal skill or knowledge to implement even complicated applications. At other installations, only limited and often unskilled assistance is available. In such cases, the user must develop and rely upon personal skills if computational resources are to be meaningfully applied, and use of that equipment for research and instruction is likely to be limited.

Access to computational resources, and the cost of that access, are governed by often rather complicated administrative rules and regulations. At some college and university installations, usually those characterized by low use of computational resources, access to the computer is free and without restriction. As demand for computational resources increases, and users begin to compete for access to those resources, regulation and, indeed, a form of rationing of access is often found to be necessary. Even the largest and most powerful hardware and software configuration has only finite capacity and cannot support unlimited use. As a result, all use is accounted for in some way, usually through the issuance of computer *accounts* and *passwords*. An account represents an acknowledged permission to use the facilities; it is usually assigned by the administrative staff of the computing center, often through a departmental representative. A password is a security technique which insures only legitimate access to whatever resources are commanded by the account. The password can and should be changed periodically by the user to whom the account was assigned.

A common practice employed to regulate and ration access is to assign monetary value to use. In such cases the computing center director, a dean or other officer, or a committee allocates to individuals dollar amounts for the purchase of computational services. The actual expenditures for services by a holder of such a computer account are entirely a function of the level and type of use of various services and their associated charges in a specific billing algorithm. Equal allocations of $100 to two individuals engaged in very different applications will undoubtedly last one user much longer than the other. This will be a function of the range of tasks to be performed and whether or not the use requires immediate access to the system. These allocations are sometimes referred to as "funny money" in that they serve only as an accounting procedure and not as a true charging mechanism in which actual money changes hands.

But whether "funny" or not, these allocations can be very real, troublesome and restrictive for users. Such an accounting system is in fact a market mechanism that can be highly restrictive where some types of application are concerned. Allocations for student use, for example, may be simply denied, or the costs assigned for usual instructional applications may be set at a level which, in relation to the total allocation, simply prohibits the use of an allotment for such applications. In setting costs for use of computational resources, a complex *billing algorithm* is sometimes employed. Differential rates are set for access to the various hardware components of the system and by varying these rates, the level of use of the various components can be changed. If, for example, demand for and use of on-line storage is high, the cost of access to disk or other on-line storage devices can be increased and the cost of access to off-line storage devices such as tape drives can be reduced. In this way, users are encouraged to limit use of on-line storage and increase use of off-line storage. The use of other hardware components can be similarly governed and adjusted. Through this market mechanism, the load on the equipment is leveled or readjusted, and the efficiency of the equipment maximized. On the other hand, a billing algorithm can be implemented in a manner that is highly prejudicial to particular kinds of applications.

The latter situation can be illustrated by considering the distinction between *batch* and *interactive computing*. In batch systems, computing jobs are part of a sequential stream and each must, in effect, wait in line for its turn to execute. In some cases, jobs are also classified and certain categories—small, or short jobs, for example—are given higher priority for processing than other classes, such as large or long jobs. In either case, the principle of first in-first out is applied either in general or within job categories. *Turnaround time* is the time that elapses between the submission of the job and the receipt of results.

Interactive computing allows much more immediate work on the basis of direct access to the available resources. In interactive systems, the user submits the job, usually employing a terminal, and execution is more or less immediate with the results quickly and directly received. Moreover, in such systems, intermediate results can be obtained; programs can be interrupted during execution and modified in terms of intermediate results; or they can be executed on a step-by-step basis with the results of each step displayed to allow the user an opportunity to select the next step or to modify the data or program as execution continues. Using a cathode ray tube terminal, for example, complex models can be displayed with appropriate coefficients derived from relevant data; the model can be modified or different data employed, and the alternative results are obtained almost immediately.

The interactive approach to computing has the obvious advantage of convenience and more or less immediate feedback. That approach also has the advantage of allowing the user to work directly with the equipment, the data, and the problem at issue. The advantages of this approach to computing for many instructional applications are equally obvious. If for no other reason, interactive computing is of value for instructional use in the immediacy of results. Using the batch approach, students must frequently wait more or less prolonged periods for results at the potential risk of loss of interest, reduced enthusiasm and diminished instructional value. The process of error correction in job submissions is often decreased in interactive processing. But there are many applications where the reduction in turnaround time is not a critical factor, and equivalent computing can be performed in a batch environment at a substantially reduced cost.

The availability of interactive computing is dependent upon the nature of the hardware and of the system software employed. It is not simply dependent upon the size and capacity of the hardware configuration as is sometimes assumed. Even very small equipment configurations can be used interactively. However, interactive computing is more demanding of machine capacity than is batch computing. Put differently, the same equipment in the same time period can execute more computing work in batch mode than in interactive mode. Moreover, batch computing can go on throughout the day including periods of low demand such as the night-time hours. In contrast, demand for interactive access is highest during the daytime hours, often referred to as *prime time*, when most users are accustomed to performing their work. To level the load on the equipment throughout the 24 hours of the day and to maximize the amount of computing that can be accomplished, billing algorithms are frequently adjusted to assign substantially higher costs to interactive than to batch computing. While the goals sought through such an adjustment are laudable and even necessary, it is often instructional applications that suffer because students then lose out on the speedy and direct interaction with the computing system.

Another way in which instructional applications may suffer is in the availability and distribution of hardware facilities, particularly in relation to the size of class enrollments. The most common problem, of course, is not having a sufficient number of terminal devices to support the demands for easy access which come from large enrollments. Many times the terminals which are available have only visual displays with no output printed on paper for students to take away for extended study. A final problem may be the location of the devices themselves, particularly on very large campuses, where social science students may have to travel some distance to concentrations of terminals which are conveniently located for students in the natural sciences. Faced with some or all of these problems, an instructor may decide that the use of the batch environment would be more effective under the circumstances.

We have discussed these essentially bureaucratic matters at such length for several reasons. In the first place, it should be emphasized that the range of research or instructional applications that can be carried out at a given installation, and the ease and efficiency with which they can be carried out, is not a simple function of the size and nature of the hardware configuration, of the nature of the system software employed, or of the available applications software. These considerations are of importance, but matters of administration and cost are often of at least equal significance. Indeed, it is certainly the case that through good management, equivalent hardware, software and expenditures at one installation can serve a user community more effectively than at another installation.

It is impossible for colleges and universities to meet rising demand for access to computational resources for increasingly diverse applications through unlimited hardware acquisition and through unlimited investment in software acquisition and development. It is also obvious that the provision of unlimited assistance and supporting personnel cannot be afforded. Decisions must be made in the expenditure of finite monetary resources, and rules must be made to govern and regulate access to computational facilities. These decisions and rules, however, are rarely designed to maximize general use or to implement an abstract principle of the greatest good for the greatest number. Rather, these procedures result in particular categories of applications and particular categories of users being encouraged while others are discouraged. In some cases, applications typical to the physical sciences are emphasized at the expense of the social sciences; research applications are sometimes emphasized at the expense of instruction and the reverse also occurs. Without invoking the familiar, and tiresome, warfare between faculty and administration, it does happen that convenience of administrative computing is sometimes given priority over research and instructional use.

But decisions bearing upon hardware acquisition, software development and acquisition, and the allocation of access to computational resources are not immutable nor are they necessarily guided by abstract rationality. The utility of scarce resources can be maximized in various ways, which is another way of saying that some receive and others do not. Many of us find ourselves, whether we like it or not, serving on departmental, division, college or university computing policy committees or in other positions from which the administration of computational resources can be influenced. In the world of college and university computing, as in other worlds, those who do not make their needs and interests known often pass unnoticed. However deplorable, it is often the squeaking wheel that is greased.

In the preceding discussion the emphasis has been upon the important elements of a computing system—the hardware, software, and administrative support required for operation. The concept of a system is derived from the necessary interrelationship of these three elements in order for computing to be possible. In the next chapter several aspects of data development and processing are presented in preparation for more detailed consideration of social science applications with these materials.

300. 183   Computational Systems 25
C 627u

BIBLIOGRAPHY—CHAPTER I   C. 1

Borko, Harold (ed.) *Computer Applications in the Behavioral Sciences.* Englewood Cliffs, N.J.: Prentice-Hall, 1967.

Clubb, Jerome M., Erik W. Austin, and Michael W. Traugott, *Computers in History and Political Science.* White Plains, N.Y.: IBM Corporation, 1972. Reprinted by ICPSR, 1976.

Janda, Kenneth. *Data Processing: Applications to Political Research.* Evanston, Ill.: Northwestern University Press, 1970.

CHAPTER II.
Data Collection

The most common educational applications of computers involve manipulation and analysis *(processing)* of data relevant to instructional and research problems and goals. Someone has wisely remarked that an egg is the first requirement for an omelette. With equally impeccable logic, the first requirement for data processing is the data themselves. Thus this chapter is concerned with the acquisition and collection of data for instructional or research applications. Succeeding chapters are concerned with data preparation and preliminary data processing, or *data management* to use conventional terminology. For these purposes, data refers in simple terms to the information to be organized, manipulated and analyzed for instructional or research purposes; processing refers to the organization, manipulation and analysis of that information.

As observed elsewhere, computer applications and the devices and procedures employed in those applications are among the most rapidly changing and developing aspects of the modern technological world. As a consequence, it is common to hear that this or that aspect of computer technology is obsolete or that better ways are now available to perform this or that task. It is also the case that among those who are deeply involved in computer applications the desire to be fully abreast of the technology is a matter of great importance. On the other hand, it is also true that access to computational facilities varies widely among institutions, and what is obsolete at one installation is *avant garde* at another. Moreover, most individuals who employ computers for research or instructional purposes are more concerned with convenience and with getting the job done than with technological currency. Thus in this chapter, as elsewhere in the present monograph, emphasis will be placed on the most common and widely employed procedures even if those procedures are not always the most technologically current. In any event, our emphasis is upon basic, conceptual elements and processes involved in the application of computers in instruction and research. While we will refer to specific devices and procedures, it should be clear that other and perhaps more advanced (or even obsolete) devices and procedures could be substituted. The basic elements and processes, however, remain substantially the same.

Datasets, Data Files and Data Matrices

Anyone who becomes involved in the application of computers to social scientific instruction and research will quickly encounter the terms *dataset* and *data file*. In practice the terms are essentially synonymous. The term dataset refers to a discrete body of computer-readable data, organized for analysis or other processing, and oriented toward a particular substantive or instructional issue, problem or phenomenon. The term data file is sometimes used to refer to the physical storage form of a discrete body of data, perhaps a portion *(subset)* of a larger dataset, on a tape or a disk. But in practice the terms are usually used interchangeably and will be so employed here.

Datasets¹ and data files are usually thought of as composed of *units of analyses* (cases) and *variables*. The units of analysis are the set of entities that constitute the subject or focus of the research, analytical, or instructional activity. As will be obvious, the units of analysis in a particular application may be the individuals interviewed in a sample survey, the nations involved in some international interaction, the counties or other geographic units or jurisdictions involved in a particular election or set of elections, the members of a Congress or Congresses, and so on. Virtually any set of entities—a class of events, a category of documents, or a population or subpopulation of individuals—can serve as units of analysis, and the units of analysis to be employed are dictated by the research problem or instructional application.

Variables can be seen as measures or indicators of characteristics or attributes of the units of analysis involved in the particular application. As will be clear, any attributes or characteristics of a set of units of analysis can be employed as variables as dictated by the particular substantive application. Variables are quantitative measures or indicators and assume a range of different values across the units of analysis. Variables, in other words, are measurements which vary in value across a set of units of analysis and can be characterized by statistical *variance*. The values for all of the variables for a particular unit of analysis constitute the elements of the *data record* for that unit of analysis. The specification of the locations of the values of variables in the record is referred to as the record *format*. When each of the variables included in a dataset is in the same location in each of the records, the dataset is described as in *fixed format*, currently the most common form of data storage for analysis.

Although these issues are discussed at greater length below, what we have described above is a rectangular data matrix. In this standard conceptualization of a dataset, information is recorded for each variable for each unit of analysis. In the actual data file, the value for each variable has the same location in the data record for each unit of analysis, and each record is of the same length. For purposes of clarity, a rectangular data matrix can be visualized in terms of Figure II-1. This is at present the most common technical form for datasets, and it is the form that is required by many, indeed most, computational systems. Two points, however, should be made clear. Datasets are not physically stored on magnetic tape or disk in this form nor are they manipulated by the central processing unit in this form. However, it is useful to conceive of datasets in this form and it is possible, if one wished, to print or list them in this form. It should also be recognized that datasets can be organized in alternative forms—in effect, in non-fixed or *free format*. Although we briefly discuss these alternative forms subsequently, they are less commonly used than the fixed format, rectangular datasets described above.

A further word is required where variables are concerned. It is useful for many purposes to think of three types of variables: identification, dependent and independent. *Identification variables* are, as the term suggests, those that are employed to identify the various units of analysis in a dataset and to distinguish one unit of analysis from another. As will be seen, identification variables can be complex and identify numerous characteristics of units of analysis, and multiple variables are required then to identify each unit uniquely. To put the matter somewhat inaccurately, *independent variables* are measures or indicators of presumed causal factors, while *dependent variables* are measures or indicators of presumed effects. A dependent variable is a measure or indicator of the phenomenon, process or characteristic to be explained in analytical terms. An independent variable, on the other hand, is a measure of a phenomenon, process or characteristic that is thought to "explain" the dependent variable.

As will be readily apparent, these distinctions are in some degree arbitrary, but they are useful for a variety of functional purposes. Variables are dependent for some substantive or analytical purposes and independent for others, and identification variables often double for some purposes as dependent or independent variables. An identification variable, for example, that identifies individuals as residents of particular states might be used as a measure of factors associated with the various states or

FIGURE II-1

Conceptual Representation of a Rectangular Data Matrix

	Variable 1	**Variable 2**		**Variable n**
Unit of Analysis 1			· · ·	
Unit of Analysis 2			· · ·	
Unit of Analysis n			· · ·	

regions which help to explain the behavior or characteristics of residents of those states.

Data Collection

In relative terms, data collection and preliminary data processing are usually the most costly aspects of research and instructional applications of computers. Once data are in error-free and appropriately organized computer-readable form, the costs of analysis and further manipulation for research or instructional purposes are relatively low. The costs of achieving that form—either monetary, in personal time, or both—are relatively high. Moreover, decisions that lead to collection and recording of inappropriate data, or to selection of inappropriate forms for organizing data, limit subsequent applications. Many more than one social scientist has invested scarce time, energy and money in collecting and processing data only to find that the data collected or the mode of organization employed did not serve the intended goals.

With these somewhat harsh realities in mind, it is only wise when beginning research or instructional projects that involve use of computers to devote adequate time and intellectual energy to planning and designing the project. In general, all elements of the project should be considered, including a clear and precise definition of the research problem or instructional goals, an assessment of available data, the identification of variables and units of analysis and the software to be used, and the selection of appropriate formats and coding conventions. Since each of these steps involve decisions, and since the human memory is fallible, all steps taken, all decisions made, and the reasons for those decisions should be recorded. As will be seen, this information constitutes the beginning of the *codebook* or *documentation* for the project and for the dataset(s) that it produces. In this section we will deal only with data collection. Subsequent sections will deal with formats and coding.

The first step in designing data collection efforts is clear, precise, and detailed definition of research problems and instructional goals. An adequate definition of problems and goals to be addressed provides a basis for identifying data requirements, for selecting appropriate units of analysis and variables, and for designing coding conventions, data formats and the organization of the data file. Without adequate definition of problems and goals, the whole data collection and preparation effort is pointless, and it should be clear that data collections can be no better than the definitions of the problems and goals which they are intended to address.

Definitions of problems and goals serves to identify data requirements. A further step—assessment of available data—is only logical. Several considerations fit under this general heading. In the first place, it is not particularly sensible to address research problems or instructional goals for which no relevant data are available. It is sometimes the case that relevant data cannot be obtained for otherwise desirable instructional or research applications, or at least not without excessive effort or expenditures beyond the means of the individual. By the same token, equipment or software required for particular applications may not be available. This is only to say that desirable applications are sometimes impractical because data or other required resources are unavailable. In some cases such problems can be circumvented, but early recognition of obstacles lessens subsequent and more grievous frustration.

In assessing the data available for a particular application it is usually useful to discover whether relevant data can be obtained in computer-readable form. As noted below, very numerous and diverse collections of readily usable computer-readable data are available from data archives, various governmental and private agencies, and other individuals. Frequently, however, researchers are unaware of the fact and collect and prepare data *de nouveau,* thus wastefully duplicating work already carried out by others. Some little effort is required to discover whether appropriate data can be obtained in computer-readable form. However, letters or telephone calls to the nationally-oriented data archives, conversations with colleagues, and examination of relevant publications will serve to locate appropriate computer-readable data or at least provide moderate assurance that a computer-readable version of requisite data is unavailable.[1]

A further consideration involved in assessing available data has to do with questions of accuracy and reliability. It is often the case that essentially similar data are to be found in several published sources. In such instances, it is obviously desirable to identify the source that is most accurate, complete and reliable. Even when data are available in only a single source, assessment of completeness, accuracy and reliability is an important and equally obvious step in data collection. In practice, a variety of more or less simple procedures can be employed to make these assessments. At the most simple level, data arrays can be scanned for unusual or missing values. It would be odd and grounds for suspicion of inaccuracy, for example, to find in a data array entries for United States counties with 100,000,000 or zero population. The cases recorded also can be counted and compared with other sources to discover whether the array is complete, and one array can be compared with another to discover whether the number and identity of cases is consistent.

Other and somewhat more complicated checks for accuracy and reliability can be carried out. Subordinate categories can be summed to superordinate categories and the resulting sums compared with recorded

---

[1] A beginning reference for this activity can be found in Jerome M. Clubb, "Sources for Political Inquiry II: Quantitative Data" as Chapter 2 in Fred I. Greenstein and Nelson W. Polsby, *Handbook of Political Science,* Vol. 7, "Strategies of Inquiry," Reading, Mass.: Addison-Wesley, 1975.

totals. Error checks such as these, of course, can be carried out more efficiently and most comprehensively after data have been converted to computer-readable form. It is sometimes useful, however, to perform such checks manually on a few cases prior to conversion to computer-readable form as a preliminary and partial test of accuracy.

In assessing data sources, the original collection and tabulation procedures and the definitions and classifications employed merit careful attention. Even sources based upon highly scientific data collection methods, such as the United States Census, are characterized by changes and variations in collection procedures and in definition and classifications. Obviously, such changes and variations must be taken into account if data are to be meaningfully employed or compared from place to place or from one time period to the other. Most investigators have encountered time series of prices, production, voter turnout or the like that are marked by pronounced shifts at particular points. Such shifts may reflect important substantive factors, but it is often the case that they result from no more than changes in data collection, tabulation or classification procedures. The preceding comments, of course, are also relevant to data collection through sample surveys. In using such data, information about the sample design, question wording, interviewing procedures and instrument design is of vital importance. Without that information, misapplications and erroneous inferences can result.[2]

But counsels of perfection are never practical. It is sometimes the case that only inaccurate, unreliable or incomplete data are available, but the research or instructional application is too important or too interesting to forego. In such cases, assessments of accuracy and reliability are particularly important. If, for example, the direction and magnitude of error or bias can be estimated, or if reasonable assumptions can be made as to their magnitude and direction, useful corrective steps, such as weighting procedures, can be systematically employed. At a minimum, assessment of accuracy and reliability provide information that can be taken into account in applying analytical procedures and in evaluating the results of those procedures. It should also be noted that assessments of the accuracy and reliability of data, of anomalies and inaccuracies that are identified, and other discrepancies should be noted and should become a part of the documentation for the data file.

Definition of the research problem or instructional goals, as suggested above, provides a basis for defining the variables and units of analysis to be employed. It is no more than a truism to say that particular units of analysis and variables are appropriate to particular problems and goals and inappropriate—indeed, meaningless and misleading—for others. In general,

[2]An extended treatment of the considerations touched upon in this paragraph can be found in Raoul Narroll, *Data Quality Control: A New Research Technique,* New York: The Free Press, 1970.

the entities about which inferences are to be drawn should constitute the units of analysis employed. If inferences are to be drawn about a population of individuals, then the individual components of that population, or a sample thereof, should be used as units of analysis. Similarly, if the focus of research or instruction is a particular category of jurisdictions—municipalities, for example—then municipalities should be used as units of analysis.

While the preceding statements appear obvious and straightforward, it is unfortunately sometimes the case that social scientists for at least superficially good reasons employ units of analysis that are not fully appropriate to the particular application. An example is provided by the use of aggregated election returns—voting returns for precincts, wards, counties, or the like—as the basis for inferences about individual voting behavior. The simple fact is that the vote cast by individuals is secret, and the only relevant information usually available is the vote aggregated to the level of geographical groups. Thus the social scientist concerned with the voting behavior of individuals must either abandon those concerns or employ aggregated voting returns for geographical units such as precincts, wards or counties. In doing so, however, the analyst risks erroneous inferences such as the well-known "ecological fallacy" unless appropriate estimation procedures are employed or the problem is reformulated.[3] In the absence of more satisfactory data, it may be necessary to employ inappropriate units of analysis, but the fact must be fully recognized in order to guard to the degree possible against the fallacious inferences that may result.

Equally simple principles can also be suggested to guide definition and selection of variables. The definition of research problems or instructional goals serves to identify concepts, relationships and explanatory factors that are critical to those problems and goals. The task is then to select variables that reflect and measure those concepts, relationships and factors as precisely and directly as possible. In selecting variables, one should give preference to basic as opposed to derived measures, to subordinate categories rather than superordinate categories, and to the component variables of summary indices rather than the indices themselves. It is not, of course, that aggregate measures, data for superordinate categories, and summary indices are without value; it is rather that raw data, component

---

[3] The seminal article on this topic is W. S. Robinson, "Ecological Correlations and the Behavior of Individuals," *The American Sociological Review*, 15 (1950), pp. 351-357. A review of these issues will be found in Leo Goodman, "Some Alternatives to Ecological Correlation," *American Journal of Sociology*, 44 (1959), pp. 610-625; Hayward Alker, "A Typology of Ecological Fallacies," in Mattei Dogan and Stein Rokkan (ed.), *Quantitative Analysis in the Social Sciences*, Cambridge: The M.I.T. Press, 1969; and W. Phillips Shively, "Ecological Inference: The Use of Aggregate Data to Study Individuals," *American Political Science Review*, 63 (December 1969), pp. 1183-1196.

variables and subordinate categories are more flexible in their analytical possibilities. If raw data are collected and recorded, aggregation can always be carried out; given subordinate categories and component variables, superordinate categories and summary indices can always be constructed. The reverse, however, is not the case.

In the preceding paragraphs emphasis was placed upon the importance of defining, selecting and employing data, units of analysis and variables that are fully appropriate to the problems and goals of particular research and instructional applications. In the most basic sense, however, these criteria can never be met. Research and instructional problems are conceptual or theoretical in nature and include as central elements such nonempirical terms as attitude, motive, cause and the like. Empirical variables and configurations of empirical data are employed as measures or indicators of these conceptual elements and the underlying phenomena. These considerations return us to matters of defining research problems and instructional goals and designing appropriate applications. Data and variables must be seen as no more than indirect measures of concepts of interest or indicators of underlying phenomena, and their strengths and weaknesses in this respect carefully assessed. The concept of "social class" provides an example of the inherent complexities in operationalization described above. There are several alternative concepts in which the researcher might be interested. These could include individuals' perceptions of their own social class, their attitudes toward the relative status of various occupations, their actual occupations, or their income levels. In actuality, when the available data sources have been searched, the researcher may find that individuals can only be characterized by an aggregated attribute of their neighborhood. These are examples of the inevitable compromises which must be made between the ideal and actual operationalizations of important theoretical concepts.

Two other matters require brief attention before turning to data preparation. As we have suggested, data collection and preparation are in relative terms the most costly elements of computer applications to instruction and research. As a consequence, data collection and preparation should be as comprehensive and as accurate as possible. That is to say, to the degree possible, all relevant data should be collected at the beginning of the project. It is always better to collect possibly redundant data than to subsequently discover that required data have been omitted and then face the tasks of relocating sources and adding or merging neglected materials to computer-readable data files. It is perhaps unnecessary to add that accurate data collection in the first instance is cheaper than to return to original sources to correct errors discovered in computer-readable files.

Data Sources

Data for instructional or research applications can often be obtained in computer-readable form from another individual or from a repository of such material. Data can also be collected by the individual from printed or manuscript sources or through other data gathering techniques such as direct observation, a personally conducted or sponsored survey, a personally administered questionnaire, or the like.

There are now numerous sources of computer-readable data. Such sources range from other individuals and groups who have collected and converted data to computer-readable form for their own research or instructional purposes through a wide variety of governmental, private, and academic agencies and organizations. This is not the place to attempt to list these various sources or to describe means of access to them. However, there are a variety of academic organizations and facilities that provide computer-readable data and other supporting resources for research and instruction in the social sciences which require special mention. These organizations and facilities are usually described as social science data archives, data libraries, or data laboratories and range from those that serve a local community of social scientists at a single college or university through a small number of large-scale, nationally, and internationally oriented organizations. Such organizations not only maintain and provide access to collections of computer-readable data but also often provide various other supporting services, including, in some cases, computer software and training and consultation facilities.

Of the major nationally or internationally oriented data archives in the United States, two can be mentioned here: the Inter-University Consortium for Political and Social Research (ICPSR) located in the Institute for Social Research of the University of Michigan and the Roper Public Opinion Research Center located at the University of Connecticut and Yale University (formerly located at Williams College). The Roper Center is the oldest nationally oriented data archive with a collection that now includes data from over 15,000 sample surveys. These surveys were originally conducted by various, but for the most part commercial, survey organizations—such as the Gallup Organization, Roper Research, and the Opinion Research Corporation—in almost 70 different countries. The earliest surveys in the collection date from the mid-1930s, and new surveys are continually being added. The Roper Center, in short, is a major repository of computer-readable commercial sample survey data.

The Inter-University Consortium for Political and Social Research is an organization of over 200 colleges, universities, research centers and institutes in the United States and a dozen or more other nations. Consortium headquarters are located in the Center for Political Studies of the Institute for Social Research at The University of Michigan. The Consortium includes among its computer-readable holdings data from a large number of sample surveys—in this case, primarily academic surveys—

conducted in the United States and various other nations. In addition to sample survey data, Consortium holdings include a variety of other computer-readable data, such as election returns for various nations; Congressional voting records, election returns and census materials for the United States from independence to the present; voting records of the United Nations General Assembly and committees; data on international events and the interactions between nations; data collections pertinent to national development and modernization; and a variety of other categories of both contemporary and historical data. The Consortium also maintains an annual summer training program in methods of empirical social research, disseminates a computer software system, and provides consultation in computer applications in the social sciences.

Data archives and other related facilities provide a means of access to data that are relevant to a variety of instructional and research applications in the social sciences. Data from these sources are supplied to the individual in computer-readable form and often in a technical form and organization that can be employed at local computer installations with little additional processing. Data archives, in short, afford in many cases a relatively simple and straightforward means to capitalize upon the advantages of computers for teaching and research.

Instructional and research applications of computers are by no means limited to the data available from social science data archives and related facilities. Original data of value for such applications are available from numerous sources. Virtually countless arrays of useful data can be found in published form, and data can also be collected through personally conducted surveys and through questionnaires administered to particular samples and populations. Indeed, the number and variety of sources of original data of relevance to research and instruction in political science are too numerous to mention here. However, it is the case that the use of data supplied by a social science data archive will eliminate the need for extensive data preparation tasks discussed in the following chapter. Most of this work is capitalized in a single effort by the archive or other data source in order to prepare and disseminate a readily usable product.

BIBLIOGRAPHY—CHAPTER II

Alker, Haywood R., Jr., *Mathematics and Politics*, New York: The Macmillan Company, 1965.

Blalock, Hubert M., Jr., and Ann B. Blalock, ed., *Methodology in Social Science Research.* New York: McGraw-Hill Book Company, 1968.

Campbell, Donald T. and Julian C. Stanley, *Experimental and Quasi-Experimental Designs for Research.* Chicago: Rand McNally & Co., 1970.

Festinger, Leon and Daniel Katz, *Research Methods in the Behavioral Sciences.* New York: The Dryden Press, 1953.

Gurr, Ted Robert, *Politimetrics: An Introduction to Quantitative Macropolitics.* Englewood Cliffs, N.J.: Prentice-Hall, Inc., 1972.

Hofferbert, Richard I. and Jerome M. Clubb, eds., "Social Science Data Archives: Applications and Potential," *Sage Contemporary Social Issues,* no. 39. Beverly Hills: Sage Publications, Inc., 1977.

Kerlinger, Fred N. *Foundations of Behavioral Research.* New York: Holt, Rinehart and Winston, 1964.

Leege, David and Wayne Francis, *Political Research: Design, Measurement and Analysis.* New York: Basic Books, 1974.

Richardson, Stephen A., Barbara Snell Dohrenwend, and David Klein, *Interviewing: Its Forms and Functions.* New York: Basic Books, Inc., 1965.

Sessions, Vivian S., ed., *Directory of Data Bases in the Social and Behavioral Sciences.* New York: Science Associates International, Inc., 1972.

Tufte, Edward. *Data Analysis for Politics and Policy.* Englewood Cliffs, N.J.: Prentice-Hall, Inc., 1974.

Vose, Clement E. *A Guide to Library Sources in Political Science: American Government.* Washington: American Political Science Association, 1975.

Webb, Eugene J. *et al., Unobtrusive Measures: Nonreactive Research in the Social Sciences.* Chicago: Rand McNally & Company, 1966.

CHAPTER III.
Data Preparation

As suggested in the previous chapter, development of procedures for conversion of data to computer-readable form is an integral part of project planning. Data files should be designed to meet and achieve project goals. In practice, inappropriately designed computer-readable files can usually be reconfigured—*reformatted*—to meet project requirements. These steps, however, are both time consuming and frustrating and can be avoided if adequate forethought is given and careful attention is devoted to details. In this chapter the focus is directed to two elements of data preparation: coding and formats. As will be noted, in some applications, aspects of this work can be carried out during the actual physical process of data collection.

Coding

In most computer applications, some coding of information is required. Coding involves the use of symbols, usually numbers, to represent characteristics, attributes, or other elements of information relevant to the particular research or instructional applications. In coding, numbers are employed to allow subsequent statistical manipulation, to capture and record elements of required information, and to meet the requirements of many software and hardware systems. Not all data, of course, require coding. Where intrinsically numeric information is concerned, actual values can and usually should be recorded. But even in the case of numeric information, coding procedures are required to record necessary identification information for units of analysis. As in all other computer applications, coding should be carefully planned and meticulously implemented, and the definitions of code categories religiously recorded.

Coding systems are sometimes simple and reflect no more than an arbitrary selection of numeric symbols to represent particular properties or characteristics of the units of analysis. It is more often the case, however, that the coding system employed is dictated by the definition of the instructional or research problem or reflects a categorization and ordering of information that is based upon a particular conceptualization or theory concerning the process or phenomenon at issue. In the latter instances, coding systems can be complex and can vary in nature from one application to the other even when the same data are employed. Viewed in these terms, coding is a form of classification; in effect, units of analysis are grouped together, or classified in terms of certain of their properties. As Meehan points out, "even a simple classification system is, in effect, a generalized structure linking together, according to similarities and differences in observed properties, a range of phenomena."[1]

An illustration of a simple and arbitrary coding system is provided by a procedure that might be used to record roll call votes in the United States House of Representatives. Here the units of analysis are the members of the House, the variables are the votes of members on (or their responses to) particular legislative issues, and the application involves investigation of the voting behavior of members of the House. On roll calls in recent Congresses, members can vote (or respond) in one of nine ways: Aye, Nay, Paired For, Paired Against, Announced For, Announced Against, Paired, Present, and Absent for the vote and no preference known. A possible coding system for these data is displayed in Table III-1.

While the preceding schema is both simple and arbitrary, it illustrates several elementary but basic principles of coding. As can be seen, application of the system to a particular vote in the House groups or categorizes members in terms of their response, those who voted Aye, those who voted Nay, and so on. The code categories employed are also both *exclusive* and *exhaustive*. As will be seen, these two criteria are sometimes difficult to meet. In the present case, however, on any particular vote, members can be assigned to one voting category and one category only. Thus the categories are exclusive. The categories are also exhaustive in that all members of a given Congress can be assigned to one or another voting category on each roll call.

As can be observed, to achieve exhaustiveness, it was necessary to employ two categories in addition to the eight that record voting responses. One of these categories ("0") was necessary to accommodate individuals whose membership either started or ended during the course of the Congress and who were, as a consequence, not eligible to vote on all roll calls in that Congress or who served as Speaker and did not customarily vote. A second category ("9") was necessary to accommodate individuals who were eligible to vote but were absent or whose vote was not recorded, probably through error, in the original source, in this case the *Congressional Record* or *The Journal of the House of Representatives*. The latter code category ("9"), it may be noted, is an example of what is usually called a *missing data code*. The information about the vote is unavailable and therefore missing. The distinction between code category "9," the missing data code, and code category "0" is obvious in the

---

[1]See Eugene J. Meehan, *The Theory and Method of Political Analysis,* Homewood, Illinois: The Dorsey Press, 1965, p. 43.

distinction between the case in which the individual in question was not a member of the House, and was not eligible to vote at the time the particular roll call occurred, and that in which the individual was eligible but not present.

For purposes of clarity, several additional aspects of this simple and arbitrary coding scheme should be noted. In the first place, only voting behavior grouped under code categories "1" and "6" counted in deciding the outcome of the roll call in question—only those categories of behavior in other words, counted in determining whether the question at issue passed, or failed. Code categories "2" and "5" indicate how "paired" individuals—members who had agreed with members on the opposite side of the issue not to vote—would have voted had they not been paired. Code categories "3" and "4" indicate how the individual would have cast his or her vote if present. Code categories "7" and "8" also indicate nonparticipation and, in a sense, the circumstances of nonparticipation but not the predisposition of the member. In one case, individuals were apparently present, could have voted, but chose not to declare a preference; in the other, the individual abstained.

Obviously, a much more simple coding scheme could be employed if only part of this information was of interest. If only, for example, the composition of the majorities and minorities that decided the outcome of the issue was of interest, members might be coded as 1 (aye), 2 (nay), and 3 (ineligible, paired, not voting, or missing data). The present schema is designed, however, to capture all, or virtually all, of the information reflected by a given roll call including the positions taken by members, the preferences of paired members, presence or absence of members, and their participation and eligibility. It is desirable at least up to a point to devise coding systems to record information in full detail rather than to collapse or truncate available information.

TABLE III-1
Hypothetical Coding System for Congressional Roll Call Votes

Form of Vote	Numerical Code Equivalent
Yes	1
Paired Yes	2
Announced Yes	3
Announced No	4
Paired No	5
No	6
General Pair	7
Present; Abstain	8
Absent or no response recorded	9
Not a member when vote was taken; or Speaker and not voting	0

Even a simple and arbitrary coding scheme, then, involves a variety of complexities of design and implementation. More elaborate coding systems are required by more complex data and problems. The example of coding occupational information is a standard means to illustrate some of these complexities. As is well known, there are literally countless specific occupations. For purposes of illustration we can imagine a lengthy series of specific occupations including physician, taxi driver, clerk, teacher, hod carrier, and so on. The series might be the occupations of members of the House of Representatives before entering Congress, the responses of a sample of the national population to a question in a census concerning occupation, or the occupational distributions of certain geographical areas. The task is to classify these occupations into categories that are meaningful in terms of the particular research or instructional application or a particular conceptual or theoretical framework. An alternative approach might be simply to list all specific occupations alphabetically and assign a unique number to each; or a unique code number might be assigned to each occupation as it appeared in the source (or sources) being employed. Such an approach is possible and might for some purposes be an appropriate way to begin to fulfill the requirements of exclusive and exhaustive categorization, but it also dodges another range of issues. At some point in the application, the specific occupations must be classified into a smaller number of categories that are conceptually or theoretically meaningful and appropriate to the particular application. Table III-2 provides an illustration of a simple classification and coding system for occupations.

As will be apparent, this example illustrates several further characteristics and problems of coding. Here again, to meet the criterion of exhaustiveness, two code categories ("6" and "9") have been employed in addition to the five substantive categories ("1" through "5") to accommodate individuals whose occupations do not fit in any of the substantive categories or whose occupations are unknown. The category

TABLE III-2
Hypothetical System for Coding Occupational Data

Occupational Classification	Numerical Code Equivalent
Unskilled	1
Skilled	2
White Collar	3
Manager	4
Professional	5
Other	6
Unknown or Missing Data	9

"9" has been designated as a missing data code. A common convention employed in coding is to reserve the value "9" as a missing data code as the upper numerical bound of possible values. Negative values ("−1" for example) are also conventionally used to indicate missing data when the variable assumes a range of real positive values. To employ this system, each unit of analysis is assigned a code value depending upon the category into which it falls. Individual units of analysis with such occupations as physician, lawyer, college professor, teacher and the like are classified as professional and assigned code value "5." This classification reveals, however, ambiguities and difficulties often encountered in meeting the criterion of exclusiveness in designing coding systems. In the present case, for example, should lawyers who work as executives in business firms be classified as professional or as managers? Obviously similar ambiguities might be encountered where the other categories are concerned.

The illustrative coding system above also involves an implicit ordinal ranking of occupations along some conceptual or theoretical dimension (or dimensions) from low (unskilled) to high (professional). What dimension is involved—whether skill, status, education, income, or other—or whether only a single dimension, is unclear. But the question of which dimension is of considerable importance. The ranking might be appropriate in terms of the dimensions of skill and education, perhaps status, but it is unlikely that it would be an appropriate income ranking. Business occupations often have higher incomes than professionals and many skilled trades are characterized by higher incomes than white collar workers.

But the point here is not to identify an accurate ranking of these occupational categories in terms of income. Rather two other matters are at issue. In the first place, while the coding scheme ranks the categories, the dimension on which they are ranked is unspecified and ambiguous. Obviously, in devising coding schemes that rank categories, the underlying dimension should be clearly specified and unambiguous. Secondly, the specific occupations that would be grouped in each of the categories are too heterogeneous to allow ranking of the categories on such a dimension as income. Thus for many purposes the hypothetical coding scheme given in Table III-2 would be inadequate.

The example is also an illustration of a severely "collapsed" coding system. An extended and detailed series of specific occupations was imagined, but these were grouped into only five categories. While these five categories might be adequate for some purposes, they also involve substantial loss of specific information which might well limit the utility of the resulting data file. There should be a general relationship between the number of units to be coded and the number of code categories to be utilized in analysis. While the research problem dictates the number of detailed categories, it is likely that a five-category scheme would be more than adequate for the analysis of a population of only 25 individuals. When samples or populations of units are quite large, however, initial care should be taken to preserve as much of the specific or detailed information provided by the original data as possible, particularly in view of the ease with which categories can subsequently be collapsed. An example of a more detailed coding system which would preserve more specific information, perhaps reduce ambiguities and still be manageable is given in Table III-3. As can be seen, the same major categories as in the earlier example have been retained, but subordinate categories have been added within each of the major categories. Obviously, the number of subordinate categories could be increased. In fact, since two digits (the last two digits) have been allocated for subordinate categories, up to 98 such categories ("01" through "98") could be used within each major category. Within each major subdivision, the value of "99" is reserved as a missing data code for those individuals whose occupation is known to fall into a given major category—unskilled, for example—but whose specific occupation is unknown. The value "999" is reserved for individuals for whom no occupational information is available.

The preceding example is also an illustration of a *nested* coding system. With occupational data coded in this fashion, the units of analysis can be grouped by using the first digit of the code into the several major categories: unskilled, skilled, white collar, manager, professional, and unknown. And by using all three digits, the units can be grouped into specific occupational categories within the major categories.

In the illustration, a single major categorization of occupations—such as unskilled, skilled, and so on—has been used. It should be clear, of course,

TABLE III-3
Hypothetical System for Coding Occupational Data

Occupation	Code	Occupation	Code
Unskilled		Manager	
Otherwise unspecified	100	Otherwise unspecified	400
Industrial	101	Salesman	401
Agricultural	102	Store owner	402
Construction	103	Supervisor	403
Other unskilled	199	Other business	499
Skilled		Professional	
Otherwise unspecified	200	Otherwise unspecified	500
Carpenter	201	Lawyer	501
Auto mechanic	202	Dentist	502
Plumber	203	Physician	503
Other skilled	299	Other professional	599
White Collar		Other	600
Otherwise unspecified	300		
Clerk	301	Unknown	999
Stenographer	302		
Accountant	303		
Other white collar	399		

that occupations can be grouped into a variety of categories along many dimensions. For some purposes, this might be a categorization of occupations as primary, secondary, and tertiary. For others, occupations might be categorized in terms of particular areas of economic activity, agriculture, industry, transportation, services, and the like. And for still other purposes the categorization might be in terms of whether or not the occupation involved ownership. In short, occupational characteristics can be coded in a variety of different ways depending upon the purposes and goals of the particular research or instructional application, and it is easy to imagine an application that would require coding data in more than one way to suit the purposes of different aspects of that application. In general, there is no single "correct" coding system for a given data collection; the appropriateness of a system depends upon the particular research or instructional goals and purposes.

A final point should be stressed even though it involves some repetition. Virtually all coding involves some loss of information. As has been suggested, coding involves grouping specific information into more general categories with the consequence of a loss of detailed information. The categorization is necessary to facilitate the analysis of patterns or trends. It is desirable to the degree possible to minimize information loss. Thus more specific coding categories are preferable to more general categories. Because classification is necessary to convert information to manageable and analyzable form, some loss of detailed information is unavoidable. It is worth remembering, however, that after data have been converted to computer-readable form, detailed code categories can be combined as needed. On the other hand, if data are recorded initially in gross categories, more detailed categories cannot be subsequently extracted and new categories cannot be created.

In most cases, data can be coded directly from original sources, whether printed documents, interview protocols, questionnaires, or other forms of recording instruments. Standardized code sheets, described below, are available for this purpose, and data are simply recorded on these sheets using predefined coding systems and formats. In carrying out coding operations, several steps can be taken to avoid error and to minimize the need for backtracking to modify coding systems that prove for one reason or another inadequate in application. *Test coding* is often useful and involves experimental coding of a segment of the data in question in order to assess the adequacy of the coding system before large quantities of data are coded. If individuals other than the principal investigator are to be employed to code data, it is usually desirable to employ several persons rather than a single coder in order to reduce the effects of individual bias. If coders are employed, careful, clear and detailed instruction and constant supervision is necessary to prevent error. Even the most diligent and dedicated coder can misinterpret or stray from instructions. *Check coding* is also often used to maintain quality control over the coding task. A sample of the already coded data is independently coded again, usually by a second coder or supervisor, and the two sets of coded data compared to detect systematic error, bias, or other discrepancies. Check coding is important in the early stages of the coding process to verify that specified procedures are understood and being followed. It is also used to maintain high quality performance until the coding phase is completed.

Formats. As was indicated above, the location of the values of variables in the records for units of analysis is referred to as the record format. As was also indicated, when the values of each variable have the same location in each record, the dataset is described as in fixed format. It is this type of format that is discussed below, although as has been seen, other types of format are also sometimes employed. A fixed format dataset is by far the most common type, however, particularly for basic applications.

It may be useful to begin the discussion of data formats by recalling the characteristics of the standard 80-column punch card. The punch card is one of those elements of data processing that is sometimes described as obsolete, and, indeed, depending upon the facilities available punched cards are often not used in recording, entering, or processing data.[2] Even so, the punch card is probably the most commonly used medium for original conversion of data to computer readable form. As will be recalled, each of the 80 columns of the punched card can be used to record the numeric digits "0" through "9" by a punch in the appropriate row for the column. Combinations of punches in each column record various "special characters" (such as "$," "%," "/," "+" and the like) and the letters of the alphabet. In many computer software systems, neither special characters nor alphabetic characters can be used for analytical purposes. Thus numeric characters are used to record data that will be the subject of analytical manipulation, while alphabetic characters are used to record information, such as the names of individuals or places, that will not be subjected to statistical manipulation.

In recording data, variables are assigned to particular columns. The number of columns assigned to a variable must be great enough to accommodate the largest value (the maximum number of digits) which the variable will assume. A variable with values that range from "0" through "9" is assigned a single column, and a variable that ranges "0" to 1,000,000 is assigned seven adjacent columns as it is not customary to record the "," in standard statistical notation. The specific columns

---

[2]In many applications where large amounts of data are to be transcribed in relatively standard formats, direct data entry techniques are finding increasing application. The devices look more like terminals than keypunches, often using CRT displays; and the data are recorded directly on magnetic tape, small reusable diskettes, or larger capacity standard disks. In addition to increased entry rates and greater flexibility in formatting, these devices often have software capabilities for intermediate data checking so that intermediate processing steps prior to analysis can be reduced or, in some cases, even eliminated.

assigned to a given variable are usually referred to as a *data field*. The card format designates the exact location of each variable, including identification as well as data variables, in terms of the specific columns to which it is assigned. In the event that more than a single card is required to record the variables for a given set of units of analysis, the location of each variable is specified in terms of both the number or order of the card on which they are located as well as the columns on the card assigned to it. Another term for the cards required to record a set of variables for the units of analysis is *deck*. The terms "card" and "deck" are often used interchangeably, as in describing the amount of data for a unit of analysis in a data file as "four decks per respondent."

These matters can be clarified by considering several illustrative card formats. For purposes of the illustration, we can imagine a hypothetical instructional or research application that involves certain aspects of the legislative behavior of the members of a particular Congress. The data to be employed are of three general types: the responses of members on roll call votes in the Congress, certain political and socioeconomic characteristics of each member's constituency, and certain biographical characteristics of each member. For purposes of the illustration, the voting response data might be seen as the dependent variables and the constituency and biographical data as the independent variables.

Figure III-4 is an example of a possible card format for recording the responses of members on roll call votes. Only one card would be required to record the information for each member of the Congress as indicated in Figure III-4. In Figure III-5 five hypothetical punched cards are displayed to illustrate the way in which the information specified in the format would actually be recorded for different members of the Congress in question. It will be recognized, of course, that the number of cards required to record this information for all members of the Congress will be equal to the total number of members, since there is one card per member.

As can be seen, the format specifies the columns allocated to each variable—both identification and data variables—and the coding conventions employed for each variable. In the case of those variables for which coding conventions are not specified, actual values would be recorded. If, for example, the data were for the Ninety-fifth Congress, "95" would be entered in columns 5 and 6. As will be noted, the actual voting responses of members are recorded in columns 31 through 80 with one column allocated to each roll call. The coding system employed is that displayed in Figure III-1 above, and the roll calls are recorded in the order that they appear in the original source, in this case the *Congressional Record*. It should be recognized that in collecting data, certain other information would be collected and recorded for each roll call to become a part of the codebook, or documentation, for the dataset. That information would include the date and subject of the roll call, the name of the individual who made the motion, and perhaps other information such as whether the motion passed or failed and the actual vote. Since all roll calls are coded in

TABLE III-4

Hypothetical Card Format for Recording Congressional Roll Call Votes

Column	Data
1	Deck Number ("1")
2	Data Type 1. Roll Call Votes 2. Constituency Characteristics 3. Biographical Characteristics
3	CHAMBER 1. House of Representatives 2. Senate
4	Senate Class (Coded 0 if House of Representatives) 1. Senate Class 1 2. Senate Class 2 3. Senate Class 3
5-6	Congress Number The sequential number of the Congress
7-8	State Code

New England
01. Connecticut
02. Maine
03. Massachusetts
04. New Hampshire
05. Rhode Island
06. Vermont

Middle Atlantic
11. Delaware
12. New Jersey
13. New York
14. Pennsylvania

East North Central
21. Illinois
22. Indiana
23. Michigan
24. Ohio
25. Wisconsin

Border States
51. Kentucky
52. Maryland
53. Oklahoma
54. Tennessee
55. Washington, D.C.
56. West Virginia

Mountain States
61. Arizona
62. Colorado
63. Idaho
64. Montana
65. Nevada
66. New Mexico
67. Utah
68. Wyoming

Pacific States
71. California
72. Oregon
73. Washington

FIGURE III-4 (continued)

Column	Data
7-8 (cont.)	State Code (cont.)

State Code (cont.)

West North Central
31. Iowa
32. Kansas
33. Minnesota
34. Missouri
35. Nebraska
36. North Dakota
37. South Dakota

External States
81. Alaska
82. Hawaii

Solid South
41. Alabama
42. Arkansas
43. Florida
44. Georgia
45. Louisiana
46. Mississippi
47. North Carolina
48. South Carolina
49. Texas
40. Virginia

9-10 Congressional District Number
Coded 00 if Senate. At-large districts are coded 98, 97, 96, etc., according to alphabetical order of the candidates. No distinction is made between various kinds of at-large districts.

11-15 Member Number
A unique five-digit number assigned to each person who has ever served in the United States Congress. The order of these numbers corresponds to the order of entries in the fourth edition of the *Biographical Directory of the American Congress, 1774-1961*, with adjustments for additional members.

16-29 Member Name
Surname first, comma, first initial if space permits. Truncate last letters of surname if longer than 14 letters.

30 Party Affiliation
1. Democrat
2. Republican
3. Independent
4. Other
9. Unknown

31 Member Vote on First Roll Call

Code	Vote
1.	Yes
2.	Paired Yes
3.	Announced Yes
4.	Announced No
5.	Paired No
6.	No
7.	General Pair
8.	Present; Abstain
9.	Absent
0.	Not a member when vote was taken; or Speaker, not voting

FIGURE III-4 (continued)

Column	Date
32	Member Vote on Second Roll Call (Coded as Column 31)
. . . .	
80	Member Vote on Fiftieth Roll Call (Coded as Column 31)

the same way, columns 33 through 80 have been omitted from the illustration in Figure III-4 in order to conserve space. However, these columns would be coded in the same fashion as columns 31, 32, and 80. If more than one card were required to record the voting responses of each member on the roll calls in the Congress, the format for these cards would be the same as Figures III-4 and III-5, except for the value of the deck numbers. The deck number for the second card for each individual would be "2," for the third "3," and so on.

In the illustration, columns 1 through 30 are assigned to identification variables. Although most of these variables are self-evident, several words of clarification are required. More than one card will be required to record the roll call, constituency and biographical data for each member. Since only a single column is allocated for deck number, it is assumed that no more than ten cards (0 through 9) will be required to record all data for each class of information. In conjunction with the column which indicates one of three types of data, the possibility exists for identifying 30 unique cards of information. The state code employed (columns 7 through 8) is another example of a nested code of the sort referred to above. The first digit allows the members to be grouped by geographic region, while the combination of the two digits allows grouping by individual states. It should be obvious, however, that a particular regionalization of the states of the nation is involved. A variety of alternative regional groupings might be employed.

In preparing the data, a unique identification number (Columns 11-15) is assigned to each member and, as can be seen, five digits have been allocated for this purpose. Thus data could be recorded for a total of 99,999 individual members. It is unlikely, however, that more than 600 individuals serve in both the Senate and House of any given Congress. The larger number makes it possible to record data for any or all Congresses using the same format and coding conventions. For purposes of visual convenience and to facilitate subsequent error checks, the name of each member is also recorded (Columns 16-29). As will be seen, some of the identification variables specified in the format that are necessary in the

FIGURE III-5
Example of the Conversion of Coded Roll Call Data to Punched Cards

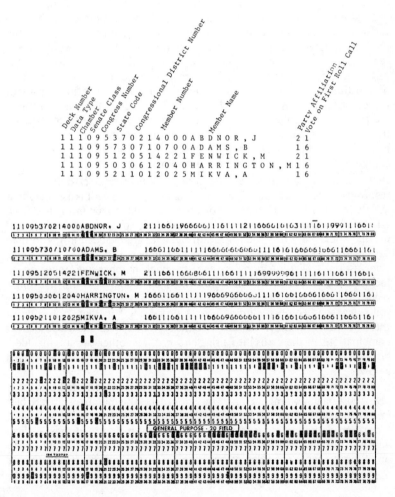

preliminary stages of processing become redundant as data work continues.

A second illustrative card format is displayed in Figure III-6, in this case to record data bearing upon the political and socioeconomic characteristics of the constituencies of members of Congress. As can be seen, the format includes the same identification variables in Columns 1 to 10 as were included in the format given in Figure III-4. These identification variables are repeated to avoid error in recording data and in order to facilitate subsequent combination of the two cards (decks) of information prior to analysis. For purposes of the illustration, provision is made for recording only a few data variables describing characteristics of the congressional district. For an actual application, additional variables requiring additional cards for each case would undoubtedly be recorded. Since these additional cards would follow the same general format as in Figure III-6, further illustration of their format is unnecessary. For the most part, the data variables are represented by measurements which are actual values rather than percentages or proportions. However, these values would allow subsequent computation of the percentages of the vote received by the candidates of the parties, the winner's margin of victory or other measures of constituency competitiveness, voter turnout, the population density of the constituency, and so on. The reason for recording the actual values rather than percentages or other derived values is, again, the greater flexibility associated with the actual values and the fact that derived measures can be calculated with greater ease and accuracy using the computer than if manual methods are employed.

To complete the present illustration, a hypothetical card format for recording biographical data is given in Figure III-7. Since it is assumed that the three cards for each member of Congress as illustrated in Figures III-4, III-6, and III-7 will subsequently be combined for purposes of analysis and manipulation, only four identification variables are included in the format. The reason for including the first (deck number) is obvious. State code, Congressional District number and member number are repeated to facilitate combination of the cards for each member to form a single record for each member. (The process of combination is discussed in the following chapter on preliminary data processing.) In fact, only one of these variables, member number, would be required to allow subsequent combinations of the cards into a single record. The other two are included, however, to provide a basis for tests of accuracy, which are also discussed below.

While the data variables included in the format are largely self-evident, a few additional comments may be in order. The number of variables included could, of course, be greatly increased and in the case of several of the variables the coding system employed is rudimentary. It may suffice, however, for illustrative purposes. It should be noted that the date of birth of each member is recorded rather than age at the time of coding. On the basis of date of birth, the age at any given date of members in any

FIGURE III-6

Illustrative Card Format for Recording Data
on the Characteristics of Congressional Constituencies

Column	Data
1	Deck Number
2	Data Type 1. Roll Call Votes 2. Constituency Characteristics 3. Biographical Characteristics
3	Chamber 1. House of Representatives 2. Senate
4	Senate Class (Coded 0 if House of Representatives) 1. Senate Class 1 2. Senate Class 2 3. Senate Class 3
5-6	Congress Number
7-8	State Code (As Figure III-5, Columns 7-8)
9-10	Congressional District Number (Coded 00 if Senate)
11	Party 1. Democrat 2. Republican 3. Independent 4. Other 5. Unknown
12-17	Vote Received in Most Recent Election 000000. Appointed to current Congress 999999. Ran unopposed, no tabulation of vote made
18-23	Vote Received by Leading Opponent in Most Recent Election 000000. Appointed to current Congress 999999. No opposition, no tabulation of vote made
24-29	Total Vote Received by "Other" Candidate(s) in Most Recent Election 000000. Appointed to current Congress 999999. Ran unopposed, no tabulation of vote made
30-36	Total Vote Cast in Most Recent Election 000000. Appointed to current Congress 999999. Ran unopposed, no tabulation of vote made
37-41	Median Income of Constituency Recorded as whole dollars

FIGURE III-6 (continued)

Column	Data
42-50	Population of Constituency
51-56	Area of Constituency Recorded to the tenth of the square mile with one implied decimal point (xxxxx.x)
57-59	Median Level of Education Recorded to the tenth of a school year with one implied decimal point (xx.x)
60-66	Population Living in Places of 10,000 or More
67-73	Population Eighteen Years of Age and Older

Congress can be calculated, and the arithmetic calculation can most accurately be made using the computer. The coding systems used to record the prior political experience of members are elementary and reflect the ambiguities of the quality of data that are typically to be found in the usual sources of biographical information. As a further reflection of those ambiguities, two essentially judgmental classifications are included in the format (Columns 23 and 39). In some cases, ambiguous data may not lend themselves to precise coding but do allow crude and tentative classification of the sort suggested. What is important in these examples is that the judgmental criteria are made explicit, allowing a reviewer of the work, or a secondary analyst, to evaluate the basis for the judgment and to consider an alternative scheme.

The coding schemes and data formats discussed above are intended as hypothetical illustrations. While formats and coding systems similar to these have been employed in actual applications, the versions presented here are truncated at a number of points in order to simplify the illustrations. The examples, moreover, relate to straightforward applications and concern only a limited number of data types. For other applications and other categories of data, significantly more complicated coding systems and data formats might be required. The illustrations are intended, however, to call attention to a few basic imperatives relative to collection and preparation of data for computer-based applications.

By no means the least important of these imperatives is the need for detailed and meticulous prior planning. This includes careful scrutiny and evaluation of available data sources and the selection of the best measures for the most appropriate units of analysis with which to pursue the substantive question at hand. This is true whether the problem involves a research exercise or the preparation of instructional materials for classroom use. Decisions made early in the process relating to the

FIGURE III-7

**Illustrative Card Format for Recording Data on the
Biographical Characteristics of Members of Congress**

Column	Data
1	Deck Number
2	Data Type 1. Roll Call Votes 2. Constituency Characteristics 3. Biographical Characteristics
3	Chamber 1. House of Representatives 2. Senate
4	Senate Class (Coded 0 if House of Representatives) 1. Senate Class 1 2. Senate Class 2 3. Senate Class 3
5-6	Congress Number
7-8	State Code (As in Figure III-4, Columns 7-8)
9-10	Congressional District Number (Coded 00 if Senate)
11-12	Congress to which First Elected
13-14	Month of Birth 01. January . . . 12. December 99. Unknown
15-16	Day of Birth 01. . . . 31. 99. Unknown
17-19	Year of Birth Code last three digits of year 999. Unknown
20	Nature of Service 1. Continuous since first election 2. Noncontinuous since first election

FIGURE III-7 (continued)

Column	Data
21	Prior Political Experience at the Local Level 0. None 1. Elective office 2. Appointive office 3. Both elective and appointive 9. Unknown
22	Prior State Office 0. None 1. Elective office 2. Appointive office 3. Both elective and appointive 9. Unknown
23	Classification of Prior Political Experience 0. None 1. Amateur (only appointive office) 2. Professional (elected to office at least once) 9. Unclassified for lack of information
24	Education 0. No formal education 1. Grade school (one to eight years completed) 2. High school (nine to twelve years completed) 3. College (one to four years completed) 4. Postgraduate education, including professional school 9. Unknown
25-27	Last College Attended 000. None, coded 0-2 or 9 in column 24

	Ivy League	**Big Ten School**
	001. Brown	101. Illinois
	002. Columbia	102. Indiana
	003. Cornell	103. Iowa
	004. Dartmouth	104. Michigan
	005. Harvard	105. Michigan State
	006. Pennsylvania	106. Minnesota
	007. Princeton	107. Northwestern
	008. Yale	108. Ohio State
		109. Purdue
		110. Wisconsin
	.	
	.	
	.	
	900. Other college or university	
	999. Unknown	

Column	Data
28-29	State of Birth (Coded as columns 7-8 above)
30-32	Primary Occupation before Entering Congress (Coded as Figure III-3 above)

FIGURE III-7 (continued)

Column	Data
33	Military Experience 0. None 1. Enlisted ranks 2. Officer 9. Unknown
34-35	Estimated Years of Prior Political Experience 00. None . . . 99. Unknown
36-38	Year of First Prior Political Office Code last three digits of year 000. None 999. Unknown
39	Estimated Income Classification of Primary Occupation Before Entering Congress 1. Low income (Lowest quartile) 2. Low middle income (second quartile) 3. High middle income (third quartile) 4. High income (upper quartile) 9. Unclassified or unknown
40	Current Congressional Office 0. None 1. Minority Whip 2. Majority Whip 3. Minority Leader 4. Majority Leader 5. Speaker
41	Committee Chairperson or Ranking Minority Member in Current Congress 0. No 1. Yes

characteristics of the data matrix are difficult and costly to change or correct at later stages of the project. Early care and attention to details will be well rewarded as actual processing of the machine-readable data gets underway.

BIBLIOGRAPHY—CHAPTER III

Cartwright, Dorwin P., "Analysis of Qualitative Material" in Leon Festinger and Daniel Katz (eds.), *Research Methods in the Behavioral Sciences.* New York: The Dryden Press, 1953.

Funkhouser, G. R. and E. B. Parker, "A Method of Analyzing Coding Reliability," in E. B. Parker et al., *Patterns of Adult Information Seeking*. Palo Alto: Stanford University Institute of Communication Research, 1966.

Holsti, Ole R., "Content Analysis" in Gardner Lindzey and Elliot Aronson, *The Handbook of Social Psychology*, vol. 2, Reading, Mass.: Addison-Wesley Publishing Company, 1968.

Muehl, Doris (ed.), *A Manual for Coders*, Ann Arbor: Institute for Social Research, 1973.

North, Robert C. et al., *Content Analysis: A Handbook with Applications for the Study of International Crisis*, Evanston, Ill.: Northwestern University Press, 1963.

CHAPTER IV.
Preliminary Data Management

With data sources identified and evaluated, data collection planned, and coding systems and data formats designed, the next steps involve conversion of data to a form that can be subjected to analysis or otherwise employed for research or instructional purposes. These latter steps involve, in general terms, the actual conversion of data to computer-readable form—the process of *data entry;* the manipulation of the computer-readable data to achieve a form suitable for the intended analysis which satisfies the requirements of the hardware and software to be employed; and implementation of certain procedures intended to identify and correct errors. In the preceding chapters some emphasis was placed on the importance of record keeping (documentation), and a section of this chapter is devoted to this matter. As was noted above, relevant data can often be obtained already in computer-readable form from a data archive, some other repository of such materials, or from another individual. In such cases, some of the work described in this and the preceding chapter is unnecessary. But additional data processing is usually highly desirable, if not always necessary, even in those cases. Hence a final section of this chapter is devoted to the use of data obtained in computer-readable form.

Data Entry

The physical process of converting data to computer-readable form is often called data entry. In discussing this process, use of the venerable card punch machine will be assumed. A variety of alternative devices and procedures are available for this purpose, including devices that involve recording data directly on magnetic tape, rather than punch cards, and *direct data entry* procedures which involve transcribing data into the storage components of the computational hardware configuration without an intermediate processing step. Despite the advantages of these devices, and still others are discussed below, they are not yet widely available or widely used. Access to keypunch machines, on the other hand, is widely available. These machines are simple to use, and, if resources permit, specially trained card punch operators usually can be employed. In general, the operations involved are essentially the same whether card punch machines, magnetic tape recording devices, or direct data entry procedures are used. Thus it is appropriate to orient the present discussion toward the keypunch machine for illustrative purposes. All of these data entry devices operate with a modified form of a typewriter keyboard, but they process cards or other storage media rather than sheets of paper. The use of the keypunch machine to convert data to computer-readable form usually involves two separate operations. In the first, data are recorded on standard 80-column punch cards according to a predesigned format and in terms of predetermined coding systems. This device actually punches the appropriate holes in the cards. Using the same data cards and formats, the second operation employs a similar machine called a *verifier*, and desirably a different operator, to test the accuracy of the transcription of the recorded data. In effect, the first operation is repeated and the characters keyed are mechanically compared with characters already punched. When the verified characters fail to correspond with those originally punched, an error signal is given and corrections can be made immediately or deferred to a later time. Essentially similar verification procedures can, and should, be employed when magnetic tape recording or direct data entry devices are used. These procedures are directly analogous to the process of check coding described above in Chapter III.

Various other error checking procedures are also often employed in the course of converting data to computer-readable form. In some cases, small samples of the punched cards are selected during the course of keypunching and are listed and visually compared with the original source. This procedure provides an additional means to identify systematic errors. As will be apparent, of course, this procedure does not serve to identify the specific location of errors. It only serves to ascertain whether a class of error is present, and the frequency with which it is present. If a class of systematic error is found to be present, a further checking procedure must be carried out to locate specific instances of that class of error. Examples of such errors would be improper reproduction or duplication of data fields or the use of incorrect formats, as well as simple invalid characters or values.

In the preceding discussions, data collection, preparation and data entry have been treated as discrete operations. In many cases, however, some of these operations can be combined. As mentioned briefly above, data can be coded directly from the original sources; and the data collection, formatting and coding operations in effect combined. For this purpose, various types of standardized code sheets are available. Typically such code sheets are divided into 80 columns, corresponding to the columns of the punch card, and contain a number of rows. One form of code sheet was illustrated in Figure I-6 on which the FORTRAN was coded. Each row can be used to transcribe, according to the appropriate format, the data to be recorded on a single punch card. Working with the code sheets, data characters are entered by the coder in each row in the column in which they are to be recorded (punched) on the 80-column card. The keypunch operator then works from the prepared code sheets in transcribing the data to machine-readable form.

Depending on the nature of the data, and the form of presentation in the original source, the intermediate step of manually transcribing data prior to keypunching may be unnecessary. In many cases, for example, copies of the relevant pages of the original source can be made. And given appropriate instructions to the card punch operator, the information can be transcribed directly from the copies of the original source to the storage medium. This approach is most practical when the original data are real numeric values and are arranged in columns and rows. It also works satisfactorily when textual information is being converted directly to machine-readable form. In practice various shortcuts can be found to combine operations and reduce effort without sacrificing accuracy.

Two other types of data entry devices merit at least brief consideration here. One of these, an *optical scanning* or *optical character recognition* (OCR) device, can be used to scan source material and automatically record that material on punched cards, magnetic tape or other storage media according to a predesignated format. These devices, however, must be programmed to accommodate the particular layout and type font used in the source documents, and in practice source materials are usually typed to prepare them for optical scanning. Unfortunately, such devices are not yet widely accessible for general use. Because they must be specially programmed for a given type font—or the information re-transcribed to another type font—they are not particularly flexible or practical for many applications. Such devices are probably most effective for relatively large-scale applications and, perhaps, particularly those that involve conversion of textual materials to computer-readable form.

The final data entry device to be mentioned actually employs a variant form of optical scanning called *mark sensing*. In the most common form, a card is employed which is formatted in the same fashion as the standard 80-column punch card, although a variety of other forms suited to various applications are also available. To record information, an individual uses a pencil to darken appropriate areas on the card or sheet. The sensing device then scans the cards or sheets so prepared, and the information is automatically recorded in computer-readable form either as punched cards or on magnetic tape or other electromagnetic media. Mark sensing devices are frequently used to process and score the responses to multiple-choice examinations. They can also prove practical, however, for research and instructional applications that involve relatively limited data of more or less consistent format.

Data Processing

In the preceding sections a series of processes were discussed culminating in the conversion of data to computer-readable form by recording information on punched cards. For some computational systems—usually those that are small and of limited capacity—punched cards are the primary data-storage medium, and data are retained on cards for subsequent processing and for research and instructional applications. It is more commonly the case, however, that punched cards are an intermediate storage medium, and data are shifted from that form to another for further processing. In either case, certain additional processing steps beyond conversion to computer-readable form are required, or at least highly desirable, before actual research or instructional work can begin. At virtually all installations general-purpose computer programs are available to carry out these operations. These programs vary in nature from one installation to the next and in many cases several of these steps can be combined and carried out in a single operation. For purposes of the present discussion, however, it is most useful to treat these procedures as discrete operations.

As suggested, punched cards are no longer commonly used as an ultimate storage medium. Magnetic tape is now the most usual primary storage medium, although magnetic disks, data cells, and other devices are also employed. Thus, the first step in data processing after conversion to computer-readable form by punching on cards is often to shift the data to another medium. This operation is frequently referred to as *reading* from cards to the other medium, as from card to tape. The translation of data recorded as holes in punched cards to binary form recorded as electro-magnetic signals was discussed in Chapter I above.

With the data on tape, further processing can be carried out with greater speed and efficiency. If the data were punched on cards as discrete data files—as in the example illustrated by Figures III-5, 7, and 8 above—the data can be *merged*, if that is desirable, to form a single integrated data file. In this operation, the three discrete types of data cards for each individual member of Congress (unit of analysis) are linked together to form a *data record* for that individual. The combination of the codes for card number and data type punched on each card is used to establish the sequence of the cards within each data record and the identification variables—member number and/or state code and district number—are used to link the appropriate cards together to form the individual data records.

This operation, then, creates a series of data records for each individual. Each new record is composed of the data originally punched on the three formerly discrete cards created for each individual. Through this process, several desirable error checks can also be carried out to ascertain whether the data matrix is complete. In order to merge data files it is usually necessary to *sort* the individual component cards into ascending or descending order in terms of the values of some identification variables. The sort operation, for which a general purpose program is available at most installations, also results in a count of the number of cards in the file. This number should, of course, be the same as the number of units of analysis involved times the number of cards of data for each unit. That is, in terms of the present example, the number of cards in each file should be equal to three times the number of members of the Congress.

The merge operation also allows further error checks to be made. In addition to the fact that there should be three card images of data present for each individual (unit of analysis) in the data file, we also know, in terms of our example, that cards which can be identified as coded "1," "2," and "3" for the variable "Data type" should also be present for each individual. At most installations general purpose programs are available to perform the merge operation and which also produce error messages if the appropriate number of cards of the appropriate designation are not found for each unit of analysis. Obviously, if the sort operation does not reveal the appropriate number of cards, or if the merge operation indicates that cards are missing or too many cards (usually duplicate cards) are present for particular units of analysis, then the precise nature of the errors should be determined and appropriate correction procedures carried out before processing continues. Usually all or part of the file must be listed and visually examined to determine the exact nature of the errors. If data are found to be missing, they must be located and added to the file; where duplicate cards are found, they must be eliminated. The process of correcting data files, it may be noted, is often referred to as *updating*, and general purpose programs to carry out these operations are also available at most installations as well.

The preceding paragraphs discussed the steps involved in creating a single integrated data file out of a series (in this case, three) discrete data files. Several error checks were also described which, given appropriate software, can be carried out in the course of executing these steps. These allow assessment of the completeness of the file and can lead to error correction procedures if discrepancies are found. The result of these steps is an integrated data file composed, to follow our example, of one data record for each member of Congress with each data record composed of three card images numbered 1, 2, and 3. To work with specific variables in a data file organized in this way, their exact card and column locations must be specified. In other words, the format notation to be used is in terms of cards and columns. The variable constituted by the second roll call vote in the Congress is located in card 1, column 32 (Figure III-4), the variable representing the population of the Congressional districts is located in card 2, columns 42-50 (Figure III-6), the variable "primary occupation before entering Congress" is located in card 3, columns 30-32 (Figure III-7), and so on.

Many of the currently available and widely used applications program packages allow very significant reduction of the complexity of card and column notation. In a step subsequent to the merge operation, programs are available to construct *logical records*, and the discrete card images are eliminated. When this procedure is employed, variable locations then become designated by character locations in a continuous string of data rather than by card and column location. In the present example, the record would be 240 characters in length (or 3 x 80 columns). Figure IV-1 gives an illustration of the translation of data locations between data records composed of discrete card images and logical records. In terms of logical records, and to continue our example, the second roll call in the Congress in question can be simply designated as located in character 31, the variable representing population of constituencies is located in characters 122 to 130, and the variable measuring primary occupation before entering Congress is located in characters 190 to 192.

FIGURE IV-1

**Translation of Data Location Specifications Between
Card Images and Logical Records**

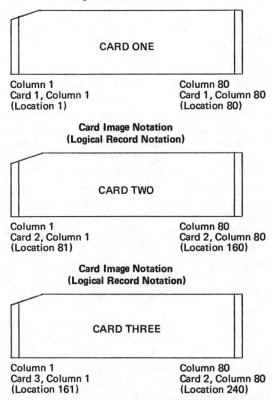

**Card Image Notation
(Logical Record Notation)**

CARD ONE

Column 1
Card 1, Column 1
(Location 1)

Column 80
Card 1, Column 80
(Location 80)

**Card Image Notation
(Logical Record Notation)**

CARD TWO

Column 1
Card 2, Column 1
(Location 81)

Column 80
Card 2, Column 80
(Location 160)

**Card Image Notation
(Logical Record Notation)**

CARD THREE

Column 1
Card 3, Column 1
(Location 161)

Column 80
Card 2, Column 80
(Location 240)

Many of the generally available computer software systems also allow additional steps which both reduce the physical size of data files and increase convenience of use. One step is to eliminate unused columns and redundant information in the original computer-readable data files in the process of creating integrated logical records. The card format specified in Figure III-4 above employed all 80 available columns; that specified in Figure III-6 used only 73 columns; and that specified in Figure III-7 used only 41 of the available 80 columns. In merging these cards to form logical records the unused columns can be eliminated to form a logical record of 194 characters as opposed to 240. Moreover, much of the identification information recorded on cards 2 and 3 in our example is redundant once logical records are formed, having been included on the original cards to facilitate record keeping and subsequent merging of the cards to form logical records. Thus, in forming logical records, the identification variables recorded in columns 1 through 10 of both card 2 and card 3 can be seen as unnecessary once the record is formed. Elimination of this data, which repeats information on card 1, further reduces the length of the resulting logical record to 174 columns as opposed to the original 240. The identification variables originally recorded on cards 2 and 3 can be safely eliminated since the creation of the logical record through the merge operation forms an integral unit which is fully identified by the identification variables originally recorded on card 1, columns 1 through 29.

Card-image data files can be readily converted to logical record files after this fashion using widely available software systems, and, indeed, some of these systems require data files in logical record form. (It should be clear, however, that such systems are not available at all installations; and card-image files remain the entry format of data almost universally.) The conversion to logical record form reduces the size of data files and, hence, reduces storage and central processing unit space requirements, both of which are at a premium at many installations. This step also at least marginally increases convenience in using data files in subsequent processing.

Various available applications software packages allow, or in some cases require, a further step which significantly increases processing convenience and efficiency. This further step involves creation of a computer-readable *dictionary* which is then associated directly with the data file which it describes. The properties of dictionary files differ somewhat from one software package to the other, and anything approaching a complete discussion of the nature and functions of dictionaries would carry us well beyond the purposes of this chapter and, indeed, beyond the purposes of the present monograph. Here it need only be noted that dictionaries represent a permanent resident description of the technical format of the associated data file. Typically, a dictionary includes machine-readable records containing such information as the sequential number of each variable in the data file which it references, the exact character location of each variable, and often a truncated name and/or description of each variable as well as certain other information bearing upon the missing data codes employed. A major advantage of this capability is that once the dictionary has been created, all subsequent references to specific variables can be made by their numbers or names. Thus, when using the data file the cumbersome and error-prone process of specifying variables by card and column or character location is eliminated. Moreover, in many software systems the dictionary capability also provides labels for tables and other results produced through analytic processing. The dictionary capability, in short, adds significantly to the ease and convenience with which computer-readable data files can be used.

We have discussed above a series of data processing steps which involve substantial modification of the form of the data as originally recorded on punched cards. It is perhaps unnecessary to note that in the process of executing these steps errors can occur which result in erasing all or part of the data file being processed or which otherwise garble the data and render them unusable. To protect against the loss of labor and investment that could result from this possibility it is usually wise to create *backup files* at each stage of processing which involves modification of the basic data format. A backup file is simply a copy of the data that can be used as a replacement should the file being processed be damaged or lost. During the initial phase of processing the original punched cards can serve as a backup file. As will be recognized, however, each of the various processing steps described above involve substantial transformation and modification of the data files. If the data files were damaged or lost after completion of some or all of these steps, significant repetition of work would be required if only the original punched cards were available as backup files. Thus, it is usually wise to create backup copies at various states of processing so that if the data files are erased or otherwise lost or damaged during a subsequent stage of processing—inadvertently *scratched* or *clobbered*, to use the jargon—the entire prior investment of labor will not be lost.

Error Checks and Correction

With these preliminary processing steps carried out, it is possible and usually desirable, to perform an additional series of computer-aided error checks and correction procedures. In the preceding sections we have stressed the need for meticulous accuracy in collecting, preparing and processing computer-readable data; and various error checking procedures—including pretesting coding systems, check coding and card punch verification—were suggested. To propose at this point still another series of error checks may seem overly elaborate, excessively demanding of time and energy, and suggestive of a virtually paranoid fear of error. It can only be noted, however, that despite the most carefully designed and meticulously executed procedures, error can occur at every stage of preparing computer-readable data files from original data collection through the various phases of data processing; and, as was noted above, original sources themselves are sometimes marred by errors and discrepancies that often cannot be detected through even the most careful visual examination.

It is also worth noting that those who employ computer-readable data for research and instructional purposes are vulnerable in particular ways. Computer-readable data are in a critical sense remote from the user. Such data cannot be easily subjected to visual examination to check the accuracy of particular sets or series of values, to ascertain that appropriate data are recorded for appropriate units of analysis, or to determine that the correct data have been recorded for given variables. In any event, visual examination of large arrays of numeric data is not a sure-fire means to identify error. Moreover, even data errors that are relatively minor from some perspectives can be compounded in statistical analysis and produce results that are seriously erroneous but detectable only with a great deal of effort. Viewed in these terms, even excessive attention to error checking and correcting can prove to be the better part of wisdom.

Several types of computer-aided error checks can be noted here, and only a little thought will suggest a variety of others. Error checking procedures are often based upon logical relationships that are intrinsic properties of the data in question. Data files are also often designed in a fashion that facilitates subsequent error checks. As an example, redundant variables are sometimes recorded for the sole purpose of later error checks. An illustration of the latter procedure was suggested above. As was noted, redundant identification variables were included in the hypothetical card formats illustrated in Figures III-5, III-7, and III-8. Either "member number" or "state code" and "Congressional District number" would have been sufficient to provide a basis for merging the three hypothetical data files. By including all three variables, however, the data could be merged using the variable "member number" and, in a subsequent operation, the accuracy of the merge checked by using the variables state code and Congressional District number. Similarly, and as might have been noted, the variable "total vote cast in most recent election" in Figure III-6 above is redundant since the value of that variable can be calculated by summing the three preceding variables. However, the total vote variable was included to allow a subsequent error check by which the computer could be used to sum the three preceding variables and to compare that sum with the recorded total vote. In this manner, the accuracy of all four variables could be assessed. Special attention would be devoted to those cases in which the difference between the keypunched total and the computer-generated sum was not equal to zero.

Still other error checks can be carried out with equal simplicity. Despite check coding and meticulous attention to coding accuracy, data can be miscoded and mistranscribed. A type of error that frequently occurs is the appearance of illegal codes—often called *wild codes*—or, in other words, the inadvertent use of code values for which no provision is made in the coding system and which, as a consequence, have no meaning. As an example, the hypothetical occupational coding illustrated in Figure III-3 and employed in Figure III-7 specifies only certain values to be used to designate particular occupations. No other values have meaning in terms of the coding system, and the appearance of a value of "114" in the data file, for example, would represent a wild code that is meaningless and an indication of error. Here again, it usually is possible to use the computer to carry out a frequency count for each variable—in other words, a marginal distribution of the frequency with which specific values appear. Obviously, if the data were accurately coded and transcribed, the frequency count should reveal only the presence of legal codes; the appearance of wild codes would indicate the presence of error and the need for remedial action.

Checks of this sort are usually not useful in the case of intrinsically numeric data—as, for example, election returns for geographical units—characterized by a wide range of legitimate values. For such data, however, the calculation of other distributional statistics often provides a useful error check. Means and minimum and maximum values can be used to identify unusual values which may indicate the presence of error.

A final set of error checks, often called *consistency* or *contingency* *checks* can be noted which capitalize upon intrinsic logical relationships characteristic of data and which can often be readily carried out using the computer. Figure III-7 provides examples of such relationships. As a general rule, one would not expect to find individuals whose primary occupation before entering Congress was coded as physician (columns 30-32) but who were also coded as without formal education (column 24). The presence in a data file of an individual coded in this fashion would be suggestive of inaccuracy. Similarly to find an individual member of Congress classified as a "professional" in terms of political experience (column 23) but for whom no prior office holding experience was indicated (columns 21 and 22) might also suggest inaccuracy.

In the case of aggregate data—election returns or population data for geographic units, for example—analogous checks can also be performed. Subordinate categories should sum to superordinate categories; the vote cast for each candidate in a given election and constituency should sum to the total vote cast in the election and constituency. By the same token, the total vote cast for President in each of the states of the union in a given election should sum to the total national vote in that election. Failure of these values to correspond would obviously be an indication of error.

In the case of survey data, there are almost always contingent relationships in the questionnaire which indicate branchings or alternative routes which the interview should take based upon specific information provided by the respondent. Sometimes this information is simply related to demographic characteristics of the respondent. Respondents who indicate they are single are not asked about the presence of children and their ages or about their spouse's occupation. In many other cases, the contingent relationships are based simply upon responses to questions of information, attitude or belief. Respondents who indicate they did not vote, for example, are obviously not asked for whom they voted. These contingent relationships are usually checked and errors corrected prior to the use of the data to make inferences about persons who voted for a certain candidate or who have families of a given size or composition.

In our discussion we have suggested a rather wide variety of possible error checking procedures that can be used to assess the accuracy of data files and to identify needed corrections. But how many such procedures are necessary? How much attention should be devoted to eliminating error? Obviously there is no single or simple answer to such questions. It will be recognized that at least for some analytical purposes, certain classes of error may not be important. In files of aggregate data characterized by large data values, for example, errors in low order digits (units or tens) do not significantly affect most analytical applications, and the effort to meticulously correct each such error may, in fact, inadvertently introduce additional and more serious errors into the file. For other categories of data and for particular applications, any error may seem intolerable, although it is difficult to imagine a data file of any magnitude that would be totally free of error. Perhaps the best answer to the question is to suggest that in preparing data, the range and number of error checking and correcting procedures that are carried out should be sufficient to provide assurance that the data are accurate enough to meet the requirements of the intended research or instructional application.

It is probably worth a brief reminder that error correction procedures should be completed before necessary derived measures are computed and before classroom or research use begins. For the purposes of most applications a variety of derived measures are required. Code values must be combined, bracketed or grouped to form new categories and variables combined to form percentages, proportions, ratios, or more complex indexes. It is obvious that derived measures can only be as accurate as the raw data on which they are based. Thus, to discover and correct data errors after such measures have been computed means that they must be recomputed after corrections to the basic data values have been carried out. Similarly, to discover data errors after analytic work has begun means that the data must be corrected and the analytic work repeated.

Data Storage

The final step in the preliminary data processing is deciding upon a storage medium for the data which facilitates subsequent analysis. The most common final storage medium is magnetic tape because it can hold a large quantity of data, takes up little space, and has a much wider tolerance for heat and humidity than cards. Tape is also relatively inexpensive, particularly when one considers it can be reused any number of times.

In the most simple and direct mode of transfer, punched cards are copied onto magnetic tape where they are recorded as electromagnetic card-images. Magnetic tape is a sequential storage medium on which the data records are recorded one after another. In actuality, the data bits are not recorded on the surface of the magnetic tape in seriatim fashion. Rather they are organized as data records with definite gaps in between to signify the difference between individual records. It is quite common for a *physical record* on tape to be the exact equivalent of a card image or it may contain a string of information which is much longer. All of the data for one unit of analysis is contained in a *logical record*. Frequently the individual data records are grouped together for more efficient storage, and the multiple of these records is called the *blocking factor*. It is quite common for there to be a hardware and/or software limitation imposed upon the maximum size of a data record, although most social science applications do not involve the manipulation or analysis of extremely large data records.

For some applications where the size of the data file is limited and cost considerations are favorable, data may be profitably stored on disk. This medium can be used for storage of data by sequential or direct access techniques. In either format, the data may be stored as card-images or as logical records just as is the case with magnetic tape. The procedures for transferring data from punched cards to disk are the same as for cards to tape. The advantage of storage on disk is quick and immediate access to the data base. It is also the case that more than one user may share simultaneous access to data stored on disk, which is not possible when a single copy of a dataset is available only on cards or magnetic tape. This difference may not be significant for individual researchers, but it greatly facilitates classroom use of computerized information by multiple students.

Documentation

At various points above we have stressed the importance of maintaining detailed records during the course of data preparation projects. These records provide the basis for what is usually called the *codebook* for the data file (or files) being created. The codebook should be seen as an evolving document which provides a continuing and detailed record of the project and contains all information necessary for effective use of the resulting data file. Upon completion of the project, the codebook should constitute a complete record of the project and a complete description of the resulting data file(s).

A distinction is sometimes drawn between the *technical* and the *substantive* documentation for a dataset. The technical documentation includes a record of the various versions of the data, including the physical characteristics of the file, and often a brief statement indicating the relationship between the dataset described and previous versions. Much of this information would be kept in a tape log or a directory of disk files. It would describe the general physical characteristics of how the tape was written and a description of the contents of each file. The latter information should include the name of the dataset, the number of records it contains, the length of each record and the blocking factor if any, and other pertinent information such as the fact that the dataset represents an exact copy of another stored in a different location or that it is the same as another but includes ten additional derived measures.

What is usually described as a codebook, however, contains the substantive documentation of the dataset in the form of descriptions of procedures, variables, and codes. Much of the desirable content of the codebook is self-evident and requires little elaboration. The codebook should include a description of the data collection procedures employed and should specify the exact sources from which particular variables were obtained. Assessments of the accuracy and reliability of sources should also be recorded along with an indication of discrepancies or shortcomings characteristic of those sources. Steps taken to reconcile or overcome discrepancies in original sources, decisions made in dealing with specific problems and ambiguities encountered in original sources, and all instances of data for specific units of analysis that could not be located should be recorded in the codebook. If sampling procedures were employed, the codebook should include a detailed description of the sample design. All data formats employed—both original, intermediate and final—should be described and all coding systems and code categories defined. If coders were employed, it is sometimes desirable to maintain a record of which data were coded by particular individuals. With this information, a class of systematic errors made more or less consistently by a particular coder could be identified, tracked down and corrected by examining all data coded by that individual.

Figure IV-2 illustrates a few sample entries from a hypothetical codebook representing the final version of the documentation for the dataset we have been using as an example since Chapter III. Although the example includes information for only three variables, it serves to demonstrate several points worth mentioning. The first entry, for variable 8, includes an indication of the sequential variable number and the character location (28) in the logical record format of the data record. The description of the variable includes a note indicating the basis for establishing party identification. And the descriptions of each code value and the category which it represents now include the distribution of the frequencies for each value across all of the units of analysis (Representatives) in the dataset. The information indicates that 292 of the total of 435 members of the House of Representatives in the 95th Congress participated as Democrats, while the remaining 143 members were Republicans.

FIGURE IV-2

Sample of Final Documentation for Dataset for 95th Congress

Variable	Location	Description
8	28	Party affiliation

This variable reflects participation in party caucuses and not the label under which the Representative was elected.

292	1. Democrat
143	2. Republican
0	3. Independent
0	4. Other
0	5. Unknown

Variable	Location	
9	29	

Election of the Speaker of the House of Representatives for the 95th Congress. The nominees were Rep. Thomas P. O'Neill, Jr. (D-Mass.) and Rep. John J. Rhodes (R-Ariz.). O'Neill was elected.

Jan. 4, 1977

Congressional Record, Vol. 123, No. 1, p. 2

290	1. Yea (vote for O'Neill)
0	2. Paired Yes
0	3. Announced Yes
0	4. Announced No
0	5. Paired No
142	6. No (vote for Rhodes)
0	7. General Pair
2	8. Present; Abstain
1	9. Absent, or no response recorded
0	0. Not a member when vote taken; or Speaker, not voting

Variable	Location	
10	30	

Motion to order the previous question (and thus end further debate and the possibility of amendment) on the House rules proposed by the Democratic Caucus.

Jan. 4, 1977   Wright (D-Texas)

CR, Vol. 123, No. 1, p. 2   Y-261   N-140

261	1. Yea
0	2. Paired Yes
0	3. Announced Yes
0	4. Announced No
0	5. Paired No
140	6. No
0	7. General Pair
0	8. Present; Abstain
32	9. Absent, or no response recorded
2	0. Not a member when vote taken; or Speaker, not voting [Representative Murphy (D-Ill.) not sworn in until January 6, and therefore not eligible to vote on this issue. All members and members-elect are eligible to vote on Speaker.]

The next variable, which contains the member's vote on the first roll call in the Congress, is located in the next sequential character location. The description of the variable includes a precis of the bill, which in this case is the vote for Speaker. The documentation for the variable also includes the date of the vote and a citation to the *Congressional Record* to indicate the source of the information. Again the marginals are included for the code categories, and they indicate the strong party voting behavior on this type of procedural roll call. Similar information is included in the description of variable 10; in addition, there is information included on who made the motion (Rep. Wright) and an indication of the outcome. Again there is a strong indication of party voting on a procedural matter, and the recorded totals virtually equal the total of "Yeas" and "Nays" with the only major differences from the total number of members being due to absences. Subsequently, on votes in which major policy issues are involved, it would be more common to find some members indicating pairings or announcements for or against a bill.

This example ends the discussion of data collection and preparation. The sample codebook for the roll call dataset illustrates the final product of this process, showing what an individual could reasonably expect to achieve in the preparation of research or instructional materials. It is important to remember, however, that there are alternative data sources, of which data archives are the prime example to be considered.

Archival Data

In recent years the practice of sharing data resources among scholars has become increasingly widespread. In growing degrees the older view that original data collected by an investigator are somehow the sole property of that investigator—to be either destroyed or husbanded and controlled in monopolistic fashion for all time—has been replaced by a more communal ethic. This ethic of sharing data is not a simple mark of generosity, but rather reflects a respect for the scientific value of replication and an interest in the cumulative goals of research. Data archives and other organizations have appeared which serve as repositories for computer-readable research data, maintain and even enhance those resources, and make them broadly available to the community of scholars for "secondary analysis." (Two such organizations, the Inter-University Consortium for Political and Social Research and the Roper Public Opinion Research Center, were mentioned in the preceding chapter.) In some cases, moreover, such organizations also carry out original collection and processing efforts, and the resulting data products become a part of a generally available store of research materials. These developments constitute a significant forward step in political science and in the other social sciences more generally. As a consequence, opportunities for scholarly use of empirical research data have greatly increased, and even undergraduate students can experience the joys—and frustrations—of working directly with major collections of empirical data.

When data are obtained in computer-readable form from a data archive, or another individual, some of the work outlined in this and the preceding chapter is obviated. That work, however, is not always entirely eliminated. Data archives, as do individual scholars, vary widely in their practices, in the procedures employed, and in their capacities for manipulating and processing computer-readable materials. Some archives can supply data as custom subsets of variables and units of analysis and in a variety of technical formats. Thus data suited to particular instructional and research interests can be obtained in technical form appropriate to the diverse and often idiosyncratic technical requirements of a local computational installation. In such cases, the data so obtained can be subjected to instructional or research use with little in the way of additional processing. The practices and technical capacities of other repositories of computer-readable data are more limited, and data can sometimes only be supplied in a single or limited number of technical forms. In such cases, more or less substantial additional processing, involving some of the steps outlined above, must be carried out to achieve a technical condition compatible with local requirements. In some instances, indeed, the additional processing required to convert the data to locally usable form may constitute a major effort so onerous as to preclude use at some installations.

By the same token, repositories differ in the attention given to organizing, documenting, checking and correcting data files (often referred to as data *cleaning*). Some data archives devote great attention to these matters; others devote little or none and maintain and disseminate data in essentially the form in which they were received from original investigators. Even then some archives may devote great attention to cleaning and documenting one data collection and virtually none to another reflecting, perhaps, assessments of the relative scholarly value and interest associated with one collection as compared to the other. Thus the secondary user may face the necessity of carrying out extensive error checking procedures along the lines indicated above. It is, of course, also worth remembering that a given data file may be "clean" enough and quite satisfactory for one research or instructional purpose but quite unsatisfactory in these terms for another. An off-hand assumption might be that a data file, while not sufficiently accurate and "clean" for purposes of serious research, would nonetheless be quite adequate for student use. Whatever is to be said of the attitudes toward students and instruction conveyed by such an assumption, it may be recalled that student interest and enthusiasm are likely to flag, and the learning experience suffer, as the frustrations of "wild" codes, illogical contingency relations, missing cases, and anomalous variables are encountered.

Documentation can also present a major difficulty, and here again practices vary. In collecting data, some investigators devote elaborate attention to recording the details of their effort from original study design through data cleaning activities. These records are then transmitted with the data to the archive and become available to secondary users. Some investigators, on the other hand, are less meticulous and rely on memory rather than a written record. By the time the data reach an archive or another individual, memory has proven fallible, and documentation is limited and inadequate. In attempting to employ such data the secondary user may find it necessary to carry out more or less extensive "preanalysis" to recapture necessary information. In the case of data collected through a sample survey, for example, it may be necessary to carry out elaborate comparisons of various sample distributions with known population distributions in order to ascertain the nature of the sampling procedures employed.

The emergence of the ethic of data sharing and the development of data archives and other repositories constitute a major boon for the study of politics and for the social sciences in general. These developments, however, do not necessarily eliminate the various activities discussed above nor do they eliminate the need for careful thought when utilizing computer-readable data for instructional or research applications. In some cases the secondary user may feel realistically confident that a given data file obtained from a particular archive is sufficiently clean and well documented that further effort of this sort would not be well repaid. In other cases, substantial processing and costly effort may be needed before data can be confidently used. The researcher should expect to receive some indication of the extent of processing performed by the archive in order to understand and anticipate any potential data processing problems which may arise.

However fortunate in some regards, the increased availability of major data collections from archives or other sources may also have a certain seductive lure for the unwary. As in the case of original data collection and processing efforts, there remains no surrogate in the secondary use of computer-readable research data for careful thought and detailed prior planning. More than one individual has rushed to acquire an important computer-readable data collection in order to pursue a particular research or instructional goal only to find, after investment of scarce time and energy, that the data were unsuited to that goal. When individuals employ data collections without sufficient regard for their properties, strengths and limitations, the results are likely to be wasted effort, frustration, and erroneous applications.

BIBLIOGRAPHY—CHAPTER IV

Anderson, Lee F., Meredith W. Watts, Jr., and Allen R. Wilcox, *Legislative Roll Call Analysis.* Evanston, Ill.: Northwestern University Press, 1966.

IBM. *Introduction to Computers in the Humanities* (G320-1044). New York: International Business Machines Corporation, 1970.

Janda, Kenneth, *Data Processing: Applications to Political Research.* Evanston, Ill.: Northwestern University Press, 1970.

CHAPTER V.
Applications Software

As defined above, the term "computer software" refers to the programs, or sets of instructions, which direct computational equipment in their operations and in the performance of specific tasks in specified ways. With no pretense to precise boundaries or definitions, a distinction was also made between systems software, on the one hand, and applications software on the other. Systems software refers to complicated instructions or programs which regulate the flow of work from one hardware component to another, establish and regulate the sequence and interrelationship of tasks to be executed, allocate work space, account for utilization, translate programs from one form (language) to another and, in general, govern and regulate the operation of the hardware configuration. Systems software can probably best be seen as an integral part of the basic computational framework which the manufacturer provides.

Most social scientists who employ computers in their work, including most of those with advanced programming skills, do not work directly with the systems software. However, the applications programs which social scientists use or write to carry out statistical or mathematical calculations, to simulate processes, or to manage and analyze data must relate to (*interface* with) the systems software. Thus the characteristics of the systems software impose constraints on applications programs and require that applications programs have particular properties and characteristics if they are to function.

This chapter is concerned with applications software. More specifically, it is concerned with the general purpose applications programs that are widely available and useful for research and instructional purposes. Such programs, for present purposes, can be grouped under two broad headings: the *utilities* software that is often written by manufacturers of computational equipment and supplied in connection with purchase or rental of that equipment; and the general purpose applications program packages developed with the needs of social scientists in mind which are now widely available. A final section is concerned with a more general discussion of the availability and nature of software support for research and instructional applications. But before considering these matters, a question of common concern to social scientists must be addressed.

Technical Expertise

In any general discussion of the use of computers in teaching and research, a question arises in one form or another as to how much in the way of technical knowledge and skill the individual must have to use these devices effectively. A major component of that question usually has to do with computer programming: in effect, must the individual know how to program in order to make use of computational resources?

As with so many other questions touched upon in this monograph, this question has no single or simple answer. It appears certain, however, that the importance of programming skills as an element of the personal arsenal of individual social scientists has been considerably exaggerated. It was once common to argue, and the view is still heard in some circles, that in the training of quantitative social scientists, proficiency in a programming language should be substituted for the requirement of proficiency in foreign languages that is a normal element of graduate programs. In our opinion, such a view is predicated upon mistaken notions of the nature and scholarly relevance of programming languages, not in keeping with the realities of the world of modern computing, and may as well reflect a mistaken notion of the general role of foreign language proficiency.

As we have observed above, the nature of the instructional and research applications that can be carried out and the efficiency and convenience with which they can be conducted using the facilities of a given installation are dependent upon the available hardware and software and the administrative and supporting structures at that installation. The characteristics of each of these components of computational systems can limit as well as enhance the kinds of applications that can be carried out. In practice, the individual who can program is sometimes able to overcome such limitations. Given requisite programming skills, even very large tasks can sometimes be carried out using equipment of very limited capacity— tasks which would be beyond the capacities of the equipment if only available general purpose software could be used. Similarly, administrative constraints upon the use of particular components of a given system can sometimes be overcome through specialized programming; and, of course, in the absence of adequate general purpose applications software and of skilled supporting personnel, possession of programming skills is of value. In general, the less well developed the computational installation, the greater the importance of personal skill and knowledge in programming and other technical areas.

An obvious advantage gained through learning programming skills is the capacity to write special-purpose programs to carry out specialized tasks or innovative applications. For those interested, for example, in process simulation or the development of instructional games, programming skill is probably of particular value. The idiosyncratic characteristics of particular data files can sometimes also require specialized programs. There are also occasions when a given computational procedure must be repeated a large number of times and a special-purpose modification of an available program can result in greater efficiency and cost savings. Although general-purpose software to carry out most statistical applications is now widely available, such programs usually employ relatively standard computational formulas and rest upon standard underlying assumptions. Should the user wish to employ variant formulas or different assumptions, special-purpose programming is often required. The capacity to write such programs, of course, facilitates methodological innovations.

These are real advantages, and their importance should not be minimized. Even so, the value of personal programming skill for most social scientists is often overemphasized. That overemphasis frequently results from failure to recognize a particular problem as an example of a class of problems for which a general procedure is appropriate and available, from a lack of information about available capabilities, or from the intrinsic interest which computer programming holds for some individuals. The latter interest cannot be faulted, but beginners particularly should have some sense of perspective in defining the difference between special problems, on the one hand, and particular applications of a general procedure, on the other. Time is often better invested in searching out and investigating available programs than in attempting to reinvent the wheel by reprogramming new capabilities. It is also worth remembering that acquisition of programming skills is not a trivial undertaking. What an amateur can accomplish in days, moreover, can frequently be done by a professional programmer in a few hours, and the quality of the product of the professional's effort is usually better.

This is not, of course, to celebrate ignorance over knowledge. It is true that given expert assistance even the most technically unwashed user can sometimes accomplish miracles of computing. For most of us, however, at least some knowledge of programming matters is desirable in order to be able to evaluate alternative software capabilities, to convey needs and deal effectively with technical personnel, and, if special programming is required, to be able to adequately describe requirements.

It is true that the use of generally available software packages limits analytical possibilities to the conventional forms of analysis. As a result there are some instances in which the ability of a social scientist to program often enables the use of more innovative techniques. Furthermore, the capacity to prepare flowcharts of the sort referred to in Chapter I is of value for these purposes and as a means to better conceptualize instructional and research applications. As in most aspects of science, it is the case that the more the researcher knows about these matters, the less likely it is that the individual will be restricted by external technical limitations.

Utilities Software

No college or university computer center is a complete desert as far as general purpose software is concerned. At a minimum, a basic set of programs, usually called *utilities*, is available at all academic computing installations. As indicated above, utilities programs are supplied by equipment manufacturers in connection with equipment purchase or rental. The nature and extent of the software provided by manufacturers varies widely. In some cases such software is limited primarily to basic data management programs—in other words, programs to read, rearrange, copy, correct, retrieve and list data—and, in fact, the term "utilities software" refers, in a strict sense, only to these capabilities. Software provided by some manufacturers, however, includes at least limited capabilities for data analysis as well.

While the extent of the software provided differs among manufacturers, and the best source of information about local availability is the computing center staff, it is generally true that some utilities are included in virtually every systems software package to carry out the basic tasks of data management. One common utilities program is used to copy from one peripheral storage device to another. A version of this program can be used to transfer data from cards to tape or to make a backup copy of a tape, and typically options are available to reblock or unblock data records as the copying takes place. In essence, groups of characters are being transferred in a sequential manner without any attention to their specific values but with the possibility of combining or separating the groups in limited ways.

A second standard utility program involves the sorting operations on data, or often the combination of sorting and merging data. In the sort operation, one or more data fields are specified as the basis for arranging the data in either ascending or descending order according to the values in those fields. There are technical conventions which designate the ordering of non-numeric characters (blanks before special characters before alphabetic characters before numerics). The essence of the sorting process is to read a record and locate the indicated field, read a second record and locate the indicated field, order the records on the basis of a paired comparison of values; and so on until the program reads the last record and locates the indicated field, and orders it on the basis of a paired comparison of all other values. The result of this operation on the data field containing member number in the example of the roll call data above would be to arrange the contents of the data file with the information for the Representative with Member Number 00001 before 00002, and so on. The sorting operation has a direct analogue in the merge function where data from two separate files, each of which is in the same sorted order, are merged together on the basis of a similar pattern of paired comparisons of values. A sorting function is available with every computer, but the speed and efficiency of the operation is directly related to the amount of direct access storage available. It is possible in small installations to perform large jobs with magnetic tapes as intermediate storage, but this involves a very time consuming and possibly expensive process.

In addition to data management capabilities, many manufacturers provide more or less extensive data analysis software as well. In most cases the statistical packages involve small discrete algorithms or subroutines for performing specific statistical operations or for computing individual statistical measures. In other instances, manufacturers are distributing statistical software developed by their user community on their own installations. The programming staff of the manufacturer adapts the software by providing the effort necessary to generalize the applications software to other hardware configurations than the one for which it was originally developed. Any search for available software at a local computing installation should include an inquiry into available data management and statistical capabilities provided by the manufacturer.

Software Packages

Although virtually all college and university computer installations have available at least limited applications software supplied by equipment manufacturers, there are significant differences in the degree of *software support* which the manufacturers provide. For various reasons, moreover, social scientists have often found manufacturer supplied software inadequate for many of their purposes. As a reflection of this dissatisfaction, very substantial human time and energy, money and other resources have been invested by individual social scientists, college and university agencies, and a variety of other organizations both public and private in development of applications software designed specifically for social scientists.

Unfortunately, the development of social science software has been characterized by considerable duplication of effort, and it is fair to say that more in the way of lip service than serious effort has been paid to cooperation and coordinated effort. In recent years, greater attention has been paid to sharing software between installations, and a variety of software capabilities are now available for purchase or acquisition through other means. While this development is of considerable benefit to social scientists there remain, as will be suggested, significant obstacles to fully generalized distribution and sharing of software resources.

As a consequence of these efforts, social scientists at most academic computing installations have access to a more or less wide range of general purpose software in addition to that provided by equipment manufacturers. These capabilities include software developed locally by individual social scientists, by the computing installation itself, or perhaps by a university, college or departmental data laboratory or other similar facility, as well as software developed elsewhere and acquired and implemented for local use. While the general purpose applications software available at local installations is too varied to permit easy generalization, these capabilities can usefully be divided into two broad and rather imprecisely demarcated categories: individual programs and program packages (or systems).

Individual programs are, as the term suggests, designed to carry out particular data processing tasks without particular regard for prior or subsequent steps. Such programs are general purpose in nature in that they are not limited to a specific and narrowly defined category of data or to data in a specific format, although the format of the input data must be defined each time such a program is used. Programs of this sort may be highly flexible in terms of the data formats which may be used, although card images are the common input format based upon the lowest common denominator principle described in Chapter I, and they may allow the user a variety of choices *(options)* as to how the particular task which they perform is to be carried out. But they are designed to execute a single task or a narrow range of tasks. And they are self-contained in terms of such matters as the input/output function, sharing no subroutines with other programs. A program to perform cross tabulations is an example of an individual program, as is a program to correct data files or to carry out factor analysis. In other words, individual programs range from those that execute very simple tasks to those that perform very complicated ones, and they can also include very elaborate options. But the program stands alone in its operation.

It may be noted in passing that to employ any program, the user must prepare a set of instructions which describes the data involved—in terms of card and column location and other properties—and specifies the options to be used in a form required by the program. These instructions are usually referred to as the *setup* for the program. Setup requirements depend primarily on the characteristics and requirements of the program and can be either quite simple or highly elaborate and complicated to prepare. One of the distinguishing characteristics of program packages, and the fact that they share many of the same subroutines, is a common structure and specification language for setups. In the case of stand alone programs, this feature, of course, would not be readily apparent because each individual program would require its own setup structure.

Program packages, as the term also suggests, are more or less integrated sets of individual programs. Although the term program system is sometimes used interchangeably with program package, the former term is also often reserved for more highly integrated capabilities while program package is applied to more loosely integrated capabilities. The distinction, however, probably need not be of concern for present purposes. The characteristics of program packages vary widely, but most allow, or require, the use of system data files (or *system files*).

When using such packages, in other words, specially organized data files are constructed with characteristics and properties that conform to the requirements of the package, and an entry program is included in the package to create such files. Program packages employ, in most cases, a shared set of input/output routines which are designed to accommodate these system files and which are common to all individual programs included in the packages. Creating standard system files is an important step in the sharing of other elements of the system capabilities. Standardized setup instructions are employed for selecting programs and program options, and this set of instructions uses a set of conventions which are applicable to all of the programs in the package. Some packages also allow, or require, dictionary information of the sort described in Chapter IV above. In short, program packages usually require additional processing steps in the initial preparation of data. However, once data are appropriately prepared, setup preparation is greatly simplified and the package provides a more convenient means to employ a more or less wide range of data management and analysis capabilities.

At many, if not most, academic computing installations, at least one locally developed program package is available. Some of these packages include only limited capabilities while others include an extended series of elaborate programs. In addition to such locally developed packages there is now a significant number of widely distributed packages which are used at many colleges and university installations. While these packages are too numerous to be considered in detail here, there are four general social science packages in sufficiently widespread use to warrant discussion.

It is likely that at least one of these systems will be available on most campuses where social science computing is performed and the size of the core memory (CPU) permits their use. Each of these systems operates primarily in the batch mode, although some intearctive capabilities are now available in the case of Conversational SPSS. All have the analogous properties of system files and a standardized setup notation (a "keyword" syntax) described above. The four systems are BMDP, OSIRIS, SAS, and SPSS. Each system actually exists in multiple versions, as some conversion efforts have taken place for hardware configurations other than IBM equipment for which each was originally designed. Each of the basic systems has a scaled-down version whereby a significant subset of the available programs run in a smaller core partition.

BMDP

The series of biomedical computer programs (BMD package) developed at the Health Sciences Computing Facility at the University of California, Los Angeles, in the early 1960s represented the forerunner in integrated software development for analytical purposes. Many present systems and programs contain algorithms from the original BMD program decks. In a 1976 release, identified as the BMDP system, this set of programs has taken on many of the system characteristics described above, including the option for system files and the use of keyword notation.[1] The BMDP system is presently composed of 26 separate statistical programs designed in six series: data descriptive programs, frequency table programs, multivariate programs, regression programs, analysis of variance programs, and special programs including data transformation programs.

The data description programs and tables in the BMDP system contain fairly standard options for describing univariate or bivariate distributions, including scatter plotting and histogram capabilities. The multivariate series includes cluster analysis, factor analysis and discriminant analysis as well as correlation programs. The regression series includes capabilities for nonlinear and polynominal regression as well as the more common options for standard and stepwise regression. There is also a special program for generating nonparametric statistics.

The system was originally written for IBM Model 360 and 370 hardware and has a minimum core requirement of 128,000 (128K) bytes of storage. The general requirement for the larger programs in the system is actually in the range of 140K to 170K. In addition to the published manual and particular documents that are delivered at the time a program tape is acquired, a periodic newsletter, "BMD Communications," is also published. The system has been modified to run on the hardware of Control Data Corporation, Honeywell, Univac, and Xerox SIGMA 7 as well.

The system programs require a rectangular card-image dataset as initial input, but there is an instruction called "SAVE FILE" which creates in effect a BMDP system file. This represents a standardized, more efficient form of internal data storage and facilitates input for subsequent operations on the dataset. The BMDP system operates essentially in a batch environment. While not truly interactive, it may be run on-line with the large IBM systems which themselves have interactive capabilities.

OSIRIS

The OSIRIS system was developed at the Institute for Social Research at the University of Michigan, as a joint venture of the Center for Political Studies and the Survey Research Center in conjunction with the Inter-University Consortium for Political and Social Research (ICPSR). It is presently in use at approximately 250 installations. The entire system is composed of 59 programs linked together by standardized input/output routines and a common keyword user language. Most of the system operates on a standard OSIRIS dataset, which is actually composed of two distinct physical data files, the dictionary file and the data file. There is an

---

[1]The most current documentation and description of the system can be found in W. J. Dixon (ed.), *BMDP Program Information* (Berkeley, Calif.: University of California Press, 1975).

entry-level program in the system which is used to construct these datasets for subsequent use.

A particular feature of the OSIRIS system is its extended data management capabilities in addition to the standard statistical software. Most of this software was developed to assist in the archival work of the ICPSR. Programs are available to deal with the conversion of data from a multiple punch to a single punch card format with only one character per column, for error checking and correcting procedures, and the merging, subsetting, and retrieval of data files in various fashions. Several capabilities are available for transforming data and aggregating records.

On the analytical side, the OSIRIS system contains all of the standard statistical techniques for dealing with univariate and bivariate distributions of variables. Special analytical capabilities include programs to evaluate response patterns among members of survey panels, four programs dealing with multivariate analysis using nominal and ordinal predictors, and several options for applying scaling techniques to data.

The OSIRIS system distributed by the Institute for Social Research and the Inter-University Consortium for Political and Social Research is designed for implementation on an IBM Model 360 or 370 computer with at least 104K bytes of available core. OSIRIS has also been converted to run on Control Data Corporation, Univac, and Siemens equipment of the appropriate size. The very largest of the programs requires approximately 200K bytes of core storage. There is an extensive six-volume documentation series available for the system, and a periodic newsletter which consists primarily of program updates is distributed to OSIRIS installations.[2] A revised version of OSIRIS is presently under development.

SAS

The SAS system was developed originally at the Department of Statistics, North Carolina State University, and the present version of the system, SAS-76, is currently in use at almost 200 installations.[3] The system contains extensive data transformation capabilities, and the setup language is structured to provide for conditional operations on the dataset. The programs require a rectangular data matrix as input, and internal SAS

---

[2]The most current documentation and description of the system can be found in the six volumes "OSIRIS III: An Integrated Collection of Computer Programs for the Management and Analysis of Social Science Data" (Ann Arbor, Mich.: Institute for Social Research, 1973). A general introduction to the system and its application is Judith Rattenbury and Paula Pelletier, *Data Processing in the Social Sciences with OSIRIS* (Ann Arbor, Mich.: Institute for Social Research, 1974).

[3]The most current documentation and description of the system can be found in Anthony J. Barr, *et al.*, *A User's Guide to SAS-76* (Raleigh, N.C.: SAS Institute, Inc., 1976).

system files can be created for subsequent analysis. What are called "programs" or "subprograms" in other systems are referred to as "procedures" in SAS.

There are 33 general procedures available in SAS-76, almost all of which involve statistical operations on the data file. A significant exception is the CONVERT procedure which can translate BMDP, OSIRIS, SPSS, or SAS-72 (the previous version) files to SAS-76 format. There is a second procedure, BMDP, which can be used to employ a BMDP program to analyze a SAS-76 dataset.

The analytical routines available in SAS-76 correspond to the set of statistical algorithms generally used with social science data. In addition to programs for producing univariate and bivariate frequencies, standard correlation and regression, and analysis of variance techniques, there are several SAS procedures which can be used for experimental design. The regression capabilities are more extensive than in any of the other packages discussed in this section. Another facility of SAS is the assembly of a variety of correlational algorithms for variables with different levels of measurement in a single procedure with extensive options. There is also a great deal of flexibility in the SAS system for custom formatting and labeling of program output, particularly tabular output.

The SAS-76 system is designed for operation in a batch environment utilizing IBM Model 360 or 370 hardware operating under the standard Operating System (or OS). It requires approximately 120K bytes of storage. The vast majority of the system is written in PL/I, with a significant proportion in assembly language and only a small amount of FORTRAN code. SAS-76 can be run under TSO (the IBM interactive operating system called *Time Sharing Option*), using the interactive capability to generate a setup for subsequent batch operation or an actual interactive run. The specific implementation of these alternatives would vary with the version of TSO operating at a particular installation.

SPSS

The most widely distributed software system available is the Statistical Package for the Social Sciences (SPSS).[4] Originally developed by social scientists in an academic setting, the system is now distributed by SPSS, Inc., and is available at approximately 800 installations in versions compatible with almost 20 different operating systems and computers. In addition to IBM hardware, the SPSS system runs on Burroughs, Control

---

[4] The most current documentation and description of the system is found in Norman H. Nie, *et al., SPSS: Statistical Package for the Social Sciences* (New York: McGraw-Hill Book Company, 1975, second edition). There is also an introduction to the system to be found in Norman H. Nie, William Klecka, and C. Hadlai Hull, *SPSS Primer* (New York: McGraw-Hill Book Company, 1975).

Data Corporation, Univac, and Xerox SIGMA-7 systems, as well as the minicomputers of the Digital Equipment Corporation and Hewlett-Packard. All of the documentation for the system is available in a single easy to understand volume.

The latest version of SPSS contains a wide variety of statistical routines and a limited but important set of data management capabilities. As a software system, SPSS utilizes a standardized control language and has an option for the generation of system files through a "SAVE FILES" instruction. The basic system operates on a data matrix of reasonable but limited size; there are larger and smaller versions of SPSS to suit particular needs or hardware configurations. The present system operates in a batch environment, although the control language resembles written text very closely. An interactive version of SPSS is presently under development which will involve a control set or specification language with even more conversational characteristics.

The number of distinct "subprograms" in SPSS is in one sense quite limited, numbering less than 20 designated items of analytical software. On the other hand, they cover the large majority of commonly employed statistical techniques and can be used in a straightforward fashion that is particularly conducive to classroom use. A second oft-cited attribute of the system is the treatment of variable names and category labels, particularly as they are used to increase the readability of the output produced by the various statistical routines.

The basic input to SPSS is a card-image dataset and a series of data definition cards, which may include the ability to save or create an internal data file. Data management facilities are provided for editing and modifying data records, retrieving subsets of variables and/or cases, and rearranging data in a file. The general analytical procedures include the treatment of distributions, correlation and regression, analysis of variance, factor analysis and scalogram analysis, and discriminant analysis.

The standard storage space requirement for SPSS is approximately 150K bytes of storage. In the standard version of the system, provision is made for 500 variables in a system file containing essentially an unlimited number of cases. There is a provision for an "archive file" which contains up to 5,000 variables, no more than 500 of which may be accessed at any given time in a given run. In the SPSS maxi-version, provision is made for a regular system file of up to 1,000 variables with the standard options for individual program treatment of numbers of variables remaining in force. Other control cards and statistical procedures operate in the same manner as in the standard version.

There is also a mini-version of the system, identified as SPSSG, which is designed for operation on relatively small systems of only 128K bytes of storage. In addition to its use on small computing systems, the SPSSG version may also have some advantages for instructional use in computing environments where the administrative arrangements and accounting algorithms relate the size of the program to turnaround time. In the mini-version the number of variables is limited to 100, no subfiles are permitted, a smaller workspace is allocated, and file modifications are generally not allowed. However, few of these considerations would be limiting factors for most classroom uses.

Each of these four software systems is widely distributed and well documented. Almost all of the commonly utilized statistical algorithms are available, methods which will prove adequate for most users in the majority of applications. Each of the packages does have its own special features and characteristics, however, particularly in the treatment of input data and the properties of individual variables, but they preclude the necessity for the individual to redesign and rewrite software to suit particular analytical needs. They are easy to use, and students can learn their operation quickly. Even researchers who customarily hire computing assistants will find much more ready access to individuals who are familiar with one or more of these major systems than to those who can quickly and effectively write appropriate special purpose software.

It is important to emphasize that one or more of these four software packages is available on most campuses. Furthermore, there are usually personnel who are particularly familiar with one of them and tend to foster its use through the quality of their consultation. The interested user should check with the computing center staff or at a social science data facility, in order to ascertain the available software and the level of support which it receives. It is generally best to follow the advice which one receives as a result of this check.

There are some broad national trends in usage which reflect preferences at a given time and are of course subject to change as the software systems themselves are modified. For example, OSIRIS has the most extensive data preparation and cleaning facilities and is often used in this fashion although analysis may be conducted using another system. SPSS is the most commonly used system for analysis because of the ease of setup, particularly the degree to which students learn it quickly. It does have relatively limited analytical capabilities, however, and many researchers turn to BMDP, OSIRIS, or SAS-76 for special procedures.

Figure V-1 presents a generalized summary of the program features of the four systems which indicates the broad range of capabilities. The information is divided into two sections to distinguish between data management and data analysis capabilities. It cannot be overemphasized that the table presents only a summary of capabilities. While the figure indicates that all four of the systems have programs with output that includes measures of association for contingency tables, for example, the limitations of space preclude a complete listing of all of the statistics which are available from each. Similarly, all of the systems have a capability for stepwise regression, but only BMDP and SAS-76 include an option for the deletion of variables one at a time (backwards stepwise) in addition to the standard procedure of adding one variable at a time. Individuals who are interested in detailed information about specific

FIGURE V-1

Summary of the Program Features of Four Social Science Software Packages: BMDP, OSIRIS, SAS-76, SPSS

	BMDP	OSIRIS	SAS-76	SPSS
Data Management Procedures				
Creation of system files	X	X	X	X
Recoding of data	X	X	X	X
Subsetting of cases and variables	X	X	X	X
Listing data	X	X	X	X
Sorting and merging data		X	X	
Correcting data values		X	X	X
Aggregating data records		X		X
Contrived data generation		X		
Randomized plan generation for experiments			X	
Conversion of multiple-punched cards		X		
Machine-readable documentation processing		X		X
Data Analysis Procedures				
Univariate frequency generation and summary statistics	X	X	X	X
Contingency tables and related measures of association	X	X	X	X
Scatter plots	X	X	X	X
Analysis of variance	X	X	X	X
Test for differences in sample means	X	X	X	X
Product-moment correlations	X	X	X	X
Partial correlations	X	X	X	X
Multiple regression	X	X	X	X
Discriminant analysis	X		X	X
Factor analysis	X	X	X	X
Cannonical correlation	X			X
Cluster analysis	X	X	X	
Time series analysis	X		X	
Guttman scaling		X	X	X
Multi-dimensional scaling		X		
Automatic Interaction Detection (AID3)*		X		X
Multiple Classification Analysis (MCA)*		X		X
Maximum likelihood (probit) analysis			X	

*These techniques for multivariate analysis using ordinal and nominal predictors were developed at the Institute for Social Research of the University of Michigan and are described in:

Andrews, F. M., Morgan, J. N., and Sonquist, J. A., *Multiple Classification Analysis* (Ann Arbor: Institute for Social Research, 1973).

Sonquist, J. A., Baker, E., and Morgan, J. N., *Searching for Structure* (Ann Arbor: Institute for Social Research, 1973).

program features should of course consult the relevant system documentation.

It is important to note at this point that the utility of a given software package in a given hardware environment is not simply a function of the size of available CPU and program size. In typical social science applications, an allowance must be made for storage of some data records as well. So the memory capacity of the computer has to be measured against the storage requirements of the program and of the *largest* (not the typical) data files in order to be reasonably certain of successful program execution.

Software Support

As we have suggested above, there is considerable difference between installations in the kind, extent and nature of available applications software. At some installations extensive software is available and a wide range of instructional and research applications can be readily implemented; at others, software is limited and instructional and research use of the computational system is more difficult. These differences reflect in part differences in the ability, or willingness, of particular installations, colleges or universities to invest in the development of applications software. And in some degree, these differences may in turn reflect the relative importance of the social sciences at particular institutions.

Sharing of computer software between installations and the distribution of generalized software packages, such as those described in the preceding section, have contributed significantly to greater equality between installations in terms of the availability of applications software. As a consequence of these efforts, many more social scientists have access to basic applications software than was the case even a few short years ago.

Moreover, distribution of such packages has also had the advantage of promoting greater standardization of social scientific computing. In the past, social scientists often encountered variations in analytical results, even when the same data were employed, as a consequence of variations in the computing formulas employed from one program to the next. Use of the same packages, of course, guarantees use of the same statistical operations, and there has also been considerable effort devoted to standardization between packages in this regard.

Acquisition of a program package or of an individual program from another installation, however, is not without cost. A purchase or rental price is involved in the case of program packages, and often in the case of individual programs as well. There is also a continuing charge for modification of the package or program, for information about errors (or *bugs*) found in the package or program, and for new versions. Moreover, program packages and individual programs must be implemented and attention must be devoted to their maintenance if they are to remain operable. Obviously, installations vary in their willingness and capacity to acquire, implement and maintain externally produced software.

We have also suggested implicitly that variations in the availability of applications software from one installation to the other are also related to considerations of hardware and systems software. The four program packages described above require equipment of middle-size or larger capacity for their implementation and at many installations the equipment available is not of sufficient capacity to employ these packages.

As we have also noted, software must be written to conform to the requirements of particular hardware and systems software. Machines produced by different manufacturers differ in their properties; and alternative operating systems are employed not only on different brands of machines, but also on machines of the same brand. The four packages described above were all originally written for IBM equipment. The original choice of that equipment was not dictated, of course, by some abstract preference for that equipment on the part of developers or by some nefarious pattern of stockholder interest. Rather, the choice was simply a reflection of the more widespread use of IBM equipment by colleges and universities, with the consequence that developers had access to that equipment and not the equipment of other manufacturers and expected the majority of subsequent use to be on that equipment as well. Fortunately, these systems have been converted for use on other equipment. We have also noted, in more general terms, that manufacturers differ widely in the degree of software which they provide. The utilities software provided by some, for example, is substantially more varied and useful than that provided by others.

The relatively recent appearance and increasingly widespread use by colleges and universities of so-called *minicomputers* has introduced a further complication where applications software is concerned. Unfortunately, the term minicomputer is seriously misleading for it is used to refer to equipment ranging from very small microprocessors usually employed for very limited and specialized applications to large machines of very substantial capacity, sometimes in the range of hundreds of thousands of bytes. In general, however, minicomputers have the advantage of providing extensive computational power for a relatively small investment. Thus they are particularly attractive for installations of limited means or where demand and need for computing resources is relatively limited. Unfortunately, development of suitable applications software, it is probably fair to say, has not yet caught up with the widespread use of this equipment. However, the manufacturers do provide software support and in many cases also support user libraries or programs which facilitate sharing of software between installations that use their equipment, and these services are certain to increase as the use of minicomputers becomes more prevalent. Some of these developments are discussed in the final chapter.

BIBLIOGRAPHY—CHAPTER V

Barr, Anthony, *et al. A User's Guide to SAS-76.* Raleigh, N.C.: SAS Institute, Inc., 1976.

Dixon, W. J., ed. *BMDP Program Information.* Berkeley: University of California Press, 1975.

Francis, Ivor and Richard Heiberger. "The Evaluation of Statistical Program Packages—The Beginning." *Proceedings of Computer Science and Statistics: 8th Annual Symposium on the Interface (1975).*

Institute for Social Research. *OSIRIS III.* Ann Arbor: Institute for Social Research, 1973.

Nie, Norman H., *et al. SPSS: Statistical Package for the Social Sciences.* New York: McGraw-Hill Book Company, 1975.

Nie, Norman, William Klecka and C. Hadlai Hull. *SPSS Primer.* New York: McGraw-Hill Book Company, 1975.

Rattenbury, Judith and Paula Pelletier. *Data Processing in the Social Sciences with OSIRIS.* Ann Arbor: Institute for Social Research, 1974.

Rowe, Beverley and Marianne Scheer. *Computer Software for Social Science Data.* London: Social Science Research Council, 1976.

CHAPTER VI.
Computer Applications in Teaching Political Science

In the preceding chapters we have suggested some technical information which is useful where either teaching or analytical applications of computational equipment is concerned. The approach has been to emphasize general concepts as they are applied to computer hardware and software and to data collection and processing. Little attention has been devoted to specific statistical techniques or analytical approaches. There are many sources of this information, either in the form of textbooks or in the substantive literature of the journals and other works which deal with these subjects more fully than could be accomplished here.

Instructional applications of computers, on the other hand, are relatively new and less widespread and much less has been written of them. As a result, some further discussion is appropriate here to introduce the reader to possibilities for the use of the computer in the political science classroom. In the discussions above, we have stressed the manipulation of machine-readable data; this is the most common but certainly not the only classroom use of the computer. We are concerned primarily with data-based approaches, because other applications such as simulation or computer-aided instruction are treated in detail in other monographs in this series. These applications are briefly described below, as well as some of the technical constraints on the instructional use of conputers.

There are several ways in which computational equipment can be utilized in conjunction with data in the classroom. At one level, they can be used to teach basic principles of research design and quantitative analysis in methodology courses. It is also clear that substantive content can also be incorporated in these exercises for instructional use in a much broader set of courses. There is quite a wide range of types of datasets or data-based exercises which are typically used for these purposes.

One example of these involves data which the instructor has collected. These materials are commonly employed in a substantive course in which the instructor has a particular research interest, and the students use the materials to replicate or extend original analysis performed by the instructor. The format of the course typically involves lectures or discussions based upon the instructor's analysis, often supplemented by other readings, with the additional data work being performed outside of the classroom.

Another source of extant data which is very similar to the first is found in the holdings of the major national or local data archives. The instructor will find several datasets which are completely documented and available in their entirety for analysis. In order to expedite classroom use, the instructor frequently creates a subset of the data and documentation for more manageable use by students. It is also increasingly the case that special instructional subsets of archival data are available.[1] The substantive context for these instructional subsets is usually major published works based upon the dataset, and the instructor has to provide guidance and consultation in the design and implementation of the exercises.

In a third variation, the class works through the complete research process on a small scale, designing and conducting their own research project. These projects often involve local surveys, but printed sources of data can, of course, be used as well. Under the guidance of the instructor, the students construct and operationalize their test of a limited theoretical model of some form of political behavior and design data collection or coding instruments. They are also responsible for all of their own data processing and analysis. In many settings this kind of activity is carried out across an entire academic year as a practicum in combination with instruction in research design and methods as well as the substantive course content.

The fourth set of materials provides a notable exception to this pattern of development of data-based instructional materials. These are books and monographs containing sequential exercises which involve the integration of substantive technical information along with the data and documentation required for assigned exercises. The initial developmental activity in this area was conducted by the Laboratory for Political Research at the University of Iowa under the auspices of several grants from the National Science Foundation. Not limited solely to the discipline of political science, manuals were developed for the use of undergraduate courses in economics, sociology, and history as well.

Each of the instructional manuals from the Social Science Curriculum Project contains a relatively brief essay which introduces the reader to the general substance of the topic. The essay is followed by a series of data exercises which involve elementary hypothesis testing. There is a codebook for the accompanying dataset and a series of elementary instructions on running the requisite exercises using the SPSS system of programs. It is

---

[1]The archive of the ICPSR has recently announced the availability of ten such instructional datasets. Additional information can be obtained by writing the ICPSR, P.O. Box 1248, Ann Arbor, Michigan 48106.

possible of course to use the data-based modules with other software systems as well.

At present there are five instructional datasets in political science available from the Social Science Curriculum Project.[2] In addition, the three manuals described for use by sociologists could also be used in political science courses as well.[3] There is also one manual available in economics and one in history.[4] A majority of the instructional manuals were tested and evaluated in the classrooms of the liberal arts colleges which comprise the Iowa Regional Computer Network. They have also been adopted as part of a national experiment in transportability called CONDUIT. The CONDUIT project, also funded by the National Science Foundation, is an attempt to document and assess the problems and parameters involved in transporting a set of computer-related curriculum materials developed at one location to another site. Originally, the participating institutions included Dartmouth College, Oregon State University, the North Carolina Educational Computing Service, and the University of Texas. These materials are now available at many institutions and can also be obtained directly from the University of Iowa as well.[5]

The most recent enterprise in this area has been the development of the *Supplementary Empirical Teaching Units in Political Science* (SETUPS) by the American Political Science Association.[6] There are now 17 monographs available in two series relating to American government and comparative world politics. Each contains an essay on a specified topic of substantive interest to political scientists with related quantitative exercises directly integrated into the text. The documentation for each associated dataset is contained in the monograph which is purchased by the students, and the dataset itself is made available in a single copy to the instructor by the Inter-University Consortium for Political and Social Research under an arrangement with the APSA. The data are provided without charge in roughly the same manner as an instructor's text.

---

[2]The political science manuals include G. R. Boynton, *Citizens and the Political System;* G. R. Boynton, *Voting Behavior in the United States;* Gerhard Loewenberg, *Voting Behavior in Western Europe;* G. R. Boynton, *Regime Change in France: The Birth of the Fifth Republic;* G. R. Boynton, *Public Attitudes Toward Democracy in Post-War Germany;* and Gerhard Loewenberg, *An Undergraduate Research Project in Legislative Behavior.*

[3]These include G. R. Boynton, *The Individual in Society: Changing Attitudes Toward Integration: 1946-1972;* and *Public Reactions to Civil Disobedience.*

[4]These are Foster Mattson, *Macroeconomics;* and John G. Kolp, *The American Frontier: 1850-1880.*

[5]Detailed information about these materials can be obtained from John G. Kolp, Social Science Curriculum Project, Laboratory for Social Research, 321A Schaeffer Hall, The University of Iowa, Iowa City, Iowa 52247.

[6]Additional information about the SETUPS monographs can be obtained by writing the Director, Division of Educational Affairs, American Political Science Association, 1527 New Hampshire Avenue, N.W., Washington, D.C. 20036.

For the most part, the SETUPS exercises involve completing a specified analytical task to answer a specific question. In statistical terms the analysis rarely goes beyond the requirement for understanding the principle of a bivariate frequency table, often allowing for the application of control variables. Elementary correlation and regression are also applied in some cases. In each module there are some questions raised for consideration which would require additional unspecified analysis by students, but their use would be discretionary with individual instructors.

The SETUPS modules usually require a minimum of two weeks to complete and may be employed for a slightly longer period depending upon the pacing of the course. In actual practice, they have been used in classrooms ranging all the way from those composed of advanced high school students to beginning level graduate students who are being introduced to quantitative methods.

A secondary benefit of the SETUPS program has been the quality of the documentation of the field testing phase which was built-in from the start as an integral part of their development. Instructors who are thinking of employing SETUPS or even developing similar materials of their own can profit from consulting the reviews of the field testing process associated with SETUPS.[7] These reviews synthesize the comments of instructors who volunteered for the testing as well as the surveyed reactions of the students, who did not volunteer. There are generalized reactions to the classroom use of computerized materials as well as specific comments related to the SETUPS.

Not all of the SETUPS modules involve data-based statistical exercises. The exceptions represent a second category of supplementary classroom exercises and include Hughes' *U.S. Energy, Environment and Economic Problems* and Hoffman's *The Dynamics of Political Budgeting*.[8] Each of these monographs is accompanied by the coded software for a computerized simulation, another relatively straightforward method of learning by doing. Readers are directed to the related monograph in this series for more thorough coverage of the field.[9] That volume contains an extensive bibliography on teaching and conducting research with simulations and of sources for the acquisition of the simulations themselves.

Simulations and games are designed to represent a particular model of elements of reality based upon some theoretical perspective of the

[7]Extensive discussion of SETUPS experiences as well as descriptions and evaluations of other curricular innovations can be found in the *DEA News,* a quarterly newspaper publication of the American Political Science Association.

[8]These monographs, available directly from the American Political Science Association, are Barry Hughes, *U.S. Energy, Environment and Economic Problems: A Public Policy Simulation,* and Marvin K. Hoffman, *The Dynamics of Political Budgeting: A Public Policy Simulation.*

[9]The related monograph in this series is Charles Walcott with Anne Walcott, *Simple Simulations* (Washington: APSA, 1976).

interrelationship between those elements. In a certain sense, their use in the classroom represents just one of the many ways by which students may be introduced to the notion of formulating or testing models or hypotheses of how the political world operates. They also provide the instructor with the opportunity to illustrate in relatively vivid and personalized terms what the alternatives of operationalizing conflicting theories might be. A central element of any simulation is that the goals must be clearly stated, and the participants must know of the constraints and limitations of the model as well.

It is common to distinguish three different forms of simulations—all-computer models, man-machine interactions, and all-human interactions. All-computer models may involve a single participant who is required to establish initial parameters for the execution of the computer program. The algorithm of the program then follows a sequence of predetermined steps and arrives at a result after a specified series of iterations. The energy simulation in the SETUPS series is of this variety.

Both the man-machine and all-human simulations involve individuals adopting roles and behavior according to specified assumptions, with some dynamic element associated with the interaction of participants over time. The actual length of time required can be anywhere from less than an hour to a few days, and the elapsed time over which the total exercise occurs could be much greater. The form of interaction and feedback is often between human participants and the computer as information about actions and reactions is communicated. The human participants may not even face each other in the same classroom setting, and the exercise takes the essential form of a game. Except in the developmental stage where complex simulations are being constructed as research tools, simulations of the all-machine form are less common in political science courses.

It is easiest to depict the general character of commonly available simulations by describing the nature of the roles which the participants typically assume. In many cases, the most common role is that of public official or policymaker, including president, governor, mayor or agency head and the like. A second role is that of legislator, with one of the primary determinants of behavior being variations in constituency. A typical scenario involves the allocation of limited resources under a variety of demand situations. Another classic role is that of nation or diplomat with the international system being the arena of activity. The typical situations accommodate a wide range of international relations, with the avoidance of war a common theme.

There are other instructional applications presently available by which elaborate computer programs can be used to teach objective, substantive information in political science courses. The instruction typically takes place with the student at a computer terminal, operating in an interactive laboratory environment instead of in a classroom or lecture hall. The instructor fills the role of counselor and consultant once the course begins, although he or she, of course, may have been instrumental in the design and implementation of the learning materials in the first place.

This general pedagogical approach is commonly referred to as *Computer-Assisted Instruction* (CAI) or in a particular form as a *Personalized System of Instruction* (PSI). Both of these topics are covered extensively in other instructional resource monographs in this series, and these sources should be consulted for detailed discussions of the advantages and disadvantages of alternative applications of these techniques.[10] Again, the purpose of the discussion which follows is only to introduce the reader to these possibilities and perhaps provide encouragement to pursue their potential application further.

Various CAI systems are explicitly designed to take advantage of the interactive capabilities of computers and the structured sequence of operations which is inherent in computer software. As a result, there is a direct physical limitation on the use of these methods where either an interactive computing environment is not available or the hardware configuration is not large enough to support the enrollment demands associated with a specific application. Students participating in a course being taught by CAI methods will be expected to spend a significant majority of what would otherwise have been their time in a regular classroom at a computer terminal, and these devices must be available in sufficient numbers. The interactive capability is required to provide speedy feedback without dramatically increasing the amount of time devoted to learning a given set of substantive materials in relation to traditional methods. A minor problem of the transferability of CAI programs from one campus to another is the technical differences in computer terminals produced by various manufacturers. These difficulties usually involve consultation with individuals at the local computing center.

Because any computer program represents an encoded algorithm translated into machine language, a specific CAI application can be seen as an explicit transformation of the instructor's choice of content and sequence of presentation of substantive material. To the extent the programs involve interim testing points and alternative learning paths based upon the results, then performance criteria may also be seen as an integral part of the computerized instruction as well. In essence, all of the elements of instruction associated with a CAI application are the same as those involved in a traditional classroom environment; and the instructor is faced with the same general range of decisions regarding content, readings, evaluations, and grading. The difference is that interactive computing capabilities are used to present the information in a particular fashion to

---

[10] The related monographs in the series are Ralph B. Earle, Jr. (ed.), *PSI and Political Science: Using the Personalized System of Instruction to Teach American Politics,* and Jonathan Pool (ed.), *Computer-Assisted Instruction in Political Science,* Washington: APSA, 1976.

students and, in some cases, to collect data on their performance to provide feedback to the instructor as well as the students.

It would be inappropriate to conclude from the preceding discussion that CAI techniques can be applied solely to political science courses dealing with the so-called objective elements of the discipline. Although this is a common application, it is by no means the case that queries are limited in the introductory American government course to the order of "The length of a United States Senator's term of office is...?" The method can just as effectively be applied to questions such as "Which of the following does (an author) consider to be the central role of elites in the process of public opinion formation?" In fact, one of the more widely cited and discussed applications of the CAI technique is in conjunction with a course in political philosophy taught at Dartmouth College which employs the interactive capabilities of the IMPRESS computer system.[11]

Despite this wide range of substantive developments, the wholesale dissemination and utilization of CAI techniques has been limited to those relatively few institutions which are well endowed with appropriate technical facilities. There was a brief and unfortunate period when the use of mark-sensed answer sheets to be optically scanned and graded by computer software was synonymous with computerized instructional applications and equated with large enrollments and inferior instruction. Present CAI applications bear little if any relationship to this early utilization of technology to alleviate the pressures of large classes. Rather they present an opportunity to take advantage of the latest available technology in the appropriate substantive context to provide personalized, high quality instruction in accord with individual capabilities and based upon measures of individual performance. Of course this does not imply that all instruction in political science will ultimately assume this form, but it does indicate that these techniques are probably useful in a wider range of applications than at present where the necessary technology is available.

The purpose of the preceding discussion has been to review some of the applications of computerized techniques to political science instruction. Although some of the examples were clearly related to data-based exercises, other examples were given of the use of available interactive computer technology to assist in the transmission of political science course content.

It is important to keep in mind, however, that whatever the application there are technical parameters which can limit or enhance the experience of students in utilizing the computer in the classroom. These factors can have particular significance for the introduction of the computer to beginners. As discussed above, the speed in response time and the feedback

---

[11]For a complete discussion of this see Joseph Hanis and Roger D. Masters, "Science, Revolution and Moral Corruption," *DEA News,* No. 9 (Spring, 1976), pp. S6-S7.

from an interactive computing environment may be superior attributes which provide for a more favorable learning environment. But special facilities, including terminals in sufficient numbers, must be available to take advantage of the power of the hardware without unnecessary administrative delays. And well written software and documentation should be available to avoid confusion and the resulting errors and frustration.

In a preceding chapter, the effects of other administrative factors, particularly the charging or accounting algorithms, on the use of computing resources were also discussed. In some instances interactive facilities may be available to sponsored research projects or the administration, for example, but not for teaching purposes. Or the accounting may be such that insufficient funds or time are made available during the day for student users. In these cases, the instructor will have to take the initiative in approaching the appropriate committees or administrators to pursue the reallocation of available resources in support of instructional needs.

The general trend is clearly toward the increased availability of hardware and software and better access to data resources for instructional purposes. More of these materials are available on an exchange or purchase basis than ever before, and an instructor can select from a variety of ready-to-use alternatives in much the same way as textbooks are chosen. There is no question that the computer will play an increasing role in political science instruction in the future.

BIBLIOGRAPHY—CHAPTER VI

CIRCUIT (Catalog of Instructional Resources for Computer Utilization in Teaching). Poughkeepsie, N.Y.: Shared Educational Computer Systems, Inc.

Earle, Ralph B. (ed.), *PSI and Political Science: Using the Personalized System of Instruction to Teach American Politics.* Washington, D.C.: American Political Science Association, 1975.

Greenblat, Cathy S. and Richard D. Duke, *Gaming-Simulations: Rationale, Design and Applications.* New York: Halsted Press, 1975.

Guetzkow, Harold, *et al., Simulation in International Relations.* Englewood Cliffs: Prentice-Hall, 1963.

Index to Computer Based Learning. Milwaukee: Instructional Media Laboratory, University of Wisconsin-Milwaukee, 1973.

Pool, Jonathan (ed.), *Computer-Assisted Instruction in Political Science.* Washington: American Political Science Association, 1976.

Walcott, Charles with Anne Walcott. *Simple Simulations: A Guide to the Use of Simulation/Games in Teaching Political Science.* Washington: American Political Science Association, 1976.

CHAPTER VII.
Some Futurology

Anyone who attempts to predict the future in an area as technologically complicated and as rapidly changing as the world of computing is courageous, if not foolhardy. Whether courageous or foolhardy, it seems clearly possible to forecast with at least reasonable confidence a variety of broad trends. Each of these trends has implications for academic use of computational resources. We can suggest the more obvious and more likely of these developments in an order roughly in reverse of that in which various topics were discussed in the preceding chapters.

To begin with, it can be expected that continuing attention will be directed to the development and standardization of applications software. As was already suggested, modification of some of the available applications software packages both to incorporate additional capabilities, to convert these packages to interactive form, and to increase the ease and convenience with which they can be used is already under way and will certainly continue. It is likely as well that increased attention will also be devoted to conversion of these and other packages and individual programs for use on smaller machines and on equipment produced by a broader array of manufacturers. New capabilities will be added to these and other packages as methodological, research, and instructional innovation continues. Thus the academic user can expect to have easier access to a broader array of standard capabilities suitable to increasingly diverse instructional and research applications.

To some degree, these trends may be crosscut, at least in the short term, by proliferation of the brands and types of computational equipment employed in the academic community. In particular, the increase in use of the so-called minicomputer that has occurred in very recent years is likely to continue but at a more rapid rate.[1] The lower cost of such equipment, and the continuing decline in that cost, practically assures its wider use both as the primary equipment at many colleges and

---

[1] A review of these trends can be found in a special issue of *Science,* vol. 195, no. 4283 (18 March 1977), devoted entirely to the topic of electronics.

universities and in a variety of data laboratories and other supporting facilities dedicated to social scientific applications. In the short term, increased reliance upon minicomputers may result in some confusion, increased diversity, and inequality of available capabilities where applications software is concerned. Even here, however, emphasis upon a broadened array of standardized and generally available applications software will continue. Nor will increased reliance on minicomputers interrupt movement toward increased and easier access to interactive computing facilities. As was suggested above, even rather small minicomputers can be employed interactively. Moreover, the increasing use of such equipment, coupled with a general decline in the relative cost of computational equipment, will mean cheaper access to these resources and reduction of administrative barriers to that access.

Data for research and instructional applications will grow in volume and become steadily more readily and easily available at, in relative terms, diminishing costs. Data archives will continue in their operation—whether new ones will be formed is another matter—and become an even more prominent part of the lives of social scientists and of growing importance as research and instructional resources. Processing of original data will become less complicated and less costly with the development and distribution of standardized software and with diminution of cost of access to computational equipment.

At the same time that minicomputers proliferate, there will also be a trend toward remote access to computational resources available on very large hardware systems. It is already possible and relatively inexpensive through telephonic communications to use the resources of distant installations, to process data located at those installations, and in this way to supplement locally available computational facilities. Thus networks of computers will become a practical reality, and regional or national installations are likely to specialize increasingly in particular applications and use the resources of other installations for other applications. Individuals located at even small institutions of limited means will have access through remote links to the most powerful equipment and software located elsewhere. Their institution will bear only the equipment costs of terminals and a remote job entry station, while the major hardware installation may be located hundreds or thousands of miles away. They will purchase computer time at the cost of actual use, and only a reduced administrative structure and technical staff will have to be supported by the institution.

At least in technological terms, in other words, instructional and research applications of computational resources are here to stay. Computers will enter the classroom, the library carrel and the faculty office in increasing abundance. The use of these devices will become less complicated, and applications less costly and more flexible. The only question really lies in devising ways to use these resources effectively in the service of meaningful instructional and research goals.

Glossary

The following listing contains operational definitions for a number of technical terms used in the text which may be unfamiliar to the reader. By no means does it represent an exhaustive glossary of the specialized terminology associated with the use of computers. Among the many sources which the reader may find useful in this regard are:

Meek, C. L., *Glossary of Computing Technology*, New York: GCM Information Corporation, 1972.

and

Weik, Martin H., *Standard Dictionary of Computers and Information Processing*, New York: Hayden Book Company, Inc., 1970.

A

ALGORITHM: a precise description of a process or sequence of operations required to solve a problem, usually the basis for design of a computer program.

ARRAY: an ordered arrangement of items of information, usually in the form of a table.

ASSEMBLER LANGUAGE: a computer programming language using symbolic input code which is translated into machine instructions on an item for item basis.

B

BACKUP FILE (COPY): a duplicate copy of a data file which is preserved in case the original is lost or otherwise becomes unusable. It is usually either an exact duplicate of the final version or a copy of the result of the prior processing step, enabling the final version to be recreated with one job submission.

BASIC: the acronym for a programming language called *B*eginner's *A*ll-purpose *S*ymbolic *I*nstruction *C*ode. It is a language designed to allow novices to perform interactive statistical manipulations, but which also has value for more advanced applications.

BATCH COMPUTING: the processing of a stream of jobs in a generally sequential manner in the order of submission or by other characteristics of the jobs. Once the stream is initiated, the processing order is predetermined and fixed. (Contrast with *interactive computing*.)

BILLING ALGORITHM: the set of rules by which the administrative policies established for allocating costs of a computing system are accounted on the basis of available system resources according to their use in a particular job submission.

BIT: the abbreviation of "binary digit," the smallest unit of stored information equivalent to a single element in a binary number.

BITS PER INCH (BPI): a measure of the density of information storage per unit length, usually associated with the storage capacity of magnetic tapes.

BLOCK: to group records for the purpose of conserving storage space and/or increasing the efficiency of access of processing; a group of records so constructed.

BLOCKING FACTOR: the number of physical records which have been grouped together to form a block.

"BUG": a mistake in a computer program or a set of instructions for a computer program, or a hardware malfunction.

BYTE: the smallest number of bits that can be read as a unit from memory into the computer's arithmetic and control unit by a single instruction.

C

CARD: see *punch card*.

CARD IMAGE: the electromagnetic representation on tape of the equivalent information stored on a punched card.

CARD PUNCH: an output device which records information on cards by punching holes to represent symbols according to established conventions.

CARD READER: an input device which interprets information on cards in the form of holes and translates the information storage form.

CENTRAL PROCESSING UNIT (CPU): the portion of computer hardware consisting of the arithmetic unit, the control unit, and the storage unit. It is sometimes referred to as the *main frame* of the computer, where the primary computing activity takes place.

CHARACTERS PER INCH (CPI): a measure of the density of information storage per unit length, usually associated with the storage capacity of magnetic tapes.

CHECK CODING: the process by which the original encoding of data is verified by an independent replication of the coding. It is used to train coders and also to establish the reliability of the coding.

CLEANING: the process of checking and correcting errors in a data file.

"CLOBBER": to accidentally write over or otherwise destroy a useful data or program file.

COBOL: the acronym for a programming language called Common Business Oriented Language. It is a data processing language designed for commercial data processing applications with instructions similar to business English.

CODE: (v.) to write instructions for a computer in machine, assembly, or compiler language. To convert information from one form to another.

(n.) a system of symbols for representing data or instructions in a classified but abbreviated form.

CODEBOOK: a form of documentation of a dataset which includes the complete technical and substantive description of each variable and the format for all of the variables in a dataset.

COMPILER (LANGUAGE): a powerful computer program which translates a source language into machine language. It is able to replace certain items of input with entire subroutines of expanded instructions.

COMPUTATIONAL SYSTEMS: the total environment required for computing activity which includes the physical devices, the encoded operating instructions, and computer-readable data.

COMPUTER: a device capable of accepting information, applying prescribed processes to the information, and supplying the results of processes.

CORE MEMORY: the high speed storage associated with the central processing unit of a computer.

D

DATA ENTRY: the process of transcribing data from an original textual source into machine-readable form.

DATA FIELD: the general storage location of one variable on a data record. In a specific example, it can often be described as having a width of n characters, columns, or equivalent locations.

DATA RECORD: a collection of machine-readable information that a computer program can process or produce.

DECK: a collection of punched cards or card-image equivalents encoded with machine-readable information. Cards containing data stored in a common format are described as belonging to the same deck; where multiple cards are required to store the information, they are distinguished by a deck number.

DEPENDENT VARIABLE: a variable whose value is determined by a function of one or more other variables; a measure of the effect of a process; an indicator of the phenomenon which the analyst wishes to explain.

DICTIONARY FILE: a form of machine-readable data file containing information about the format and other technical specifications of a data file. The use of a dictionary file in conjunction with a data file usually means that variables can be referred to in job submissions by number or name.

DIRECT DATA ENTRY: the process of transcribing data from an original textual source into machine-readable form that is directly accessible by computer software.

DIRECT ACCESS DEVICE: a piece of computer hardware for the storage of data on which access to a particular address is such that the time required to transfer a unit of information to or from the storage is independent of the location which is addressed. (Contrast with *sequential access device.*)

DISK: a storage device on which information is recorded on a magnetized, rotating surface. When mounted on a disk drive, this form of storage usually provides direct access to data elements anywhere on the surface, although access is also available in a sequential manner as well.

DOCUMENTATION: the complete historical record of the generation and processing of a dataset, including the codebook, information about the storage locations of the data, and the processing procedures employed.

E

EXECUTIVE SYSTEM: an operating programming system which is in control of all system functions, such as scheduling and basic input/output operations. Same as *monitor.*

F

FIXED FORMAT: a method of storing information whereby the same data element or variable occupies the same relative position in each data record. (Contrast with *free format.*)

FORMAT: a specified and predetermined arrangement of the characters in a data record.

FORTRAN: the acronym for a programming language for *for*mula *tran*slation. It is a data processing language which closely resembles mathematical notation.

FREE FORMAT: a method of storing information which does not presuppose that each data element or variable occupies the same relative position in each data record, but rather has its location designated by a delimiter. (Contrast with *fixed format.*)

H

HARDWARE: the physical equipment which comprises a computing system.

I

IDENTIFICATION VARIABLE: an item of information which in itself or in combination with others can be used to identify uniquely a data record.

INDEPENDENT VARIABLE: a variable whose value determines the value of another variable; a measure of the cause of a process.

INTERACTIVE COMPUTING: the processing of data on a real time basis so that the results are available in time to influence or alter the actual process itself under control of the user. (Contrast with *batch computing.*)

INTERFACE: (n.) a common boundary or interconnection between two pieces of computing equipment;

(v.) to develop or program a common interconnection between two pieces of equipment or two software systems.

INTERBLOK GAP: the unrecorded portion between blocks on a magnetic tape.

"I/O": an abbreviation for input/output, a general term for the process or devices used to get information into and out of a computing system.

K

"K": an abbreviation in the metric system which denotes 1000. The precise meaning in reference to computer storage capacities is 1,024 (or 2 to the 10th power).

KEYPUNCH: (n.) a device for transcribing data in textual form to a computer-readable format by the punching of holes in a card in a specified manner.

(v.) to transcribe information to computer-readable form employing a keypunch machine.

L

LINE PRINTER: an output device which prints information one entire line at a time, as opposed to a single character at a time, by means of an element which contains as many print positions as an output page.

LOGICAL RECORD: the collection of all of the data for a given unit of analysis which is treated as a conceptual entity. It is distinguished from a *physical record,* more than one of which may be required to store the information for a logical record.

M

MACHINE LANGUAGE: a programming language designed for interpretation and use by a machine without translation, usually expressed in the number system basic to a computer.

MAGNETIC TAPE: a data storage medium consisting of a plastic material with an electromagnetic coating on which binary data are stored as magnetized spots in column form across the width of the tape.

MARK SENSING: a data transcription technique by which preformatted marks on special forms are recognized and converted to machine-readable data.

MERGE: to combine data records in an ordered fashion based upon a common characteristic, usually the value(s) of equivalent variables.

MONITOR: an operating programming system which is in control of all system functions, such as scheduling and basic input/output operations. Same as *executive system*.

O

OFF-LINE PROCESSING: the processing of data on peripheral devices away from the main frame of the computer.

ON-LINE PROCESSING: the processing of data on the main frame of the computer, often in such a fashion that the results of the processing are directly useful to the actual operation.

OPTICAL CHARACTER READER/RECOGNITION (OCR): a device which recognizes printed characters in special fonts by their images and translates that information into machine-readable form. The process of reading printed data and translating it into machine-readable form.

P

PAPER TAPE PUNCH/READER: a device for the input or output of data stored in a sequential fashion as a series of holes in a roll of paper tape.

PERIPHERAL: a piece of computer hardware separate from but connected to the main computer. Peripheral devices are typically used for additional storage and for input/output functions.

PHYSICAL RECORD: a discrete collection of machine-readable information, usually associated with a single unit of analysis, which is a readily identifiable unit of storage and retrieval.

PL/1: the acronym for a programming language called *P*rogramming *L*anguage 1. It is a language with capabilities similar to FORTRAN but designed to have simpler conventions for coding instructions.

"PRIME TIME": the time(s) of day when demand for computing resources is greatest, usually during the standard working hours. Many local charging policies associate a premium with computing resources during this period in order to encourage use at alternative times.

PUNCH CARD: a data storage medium on which information is represented by a series of holes in a predetermined sequence. One or more punches may appear in any of 12 rows distributed across 80 columns on the surface of the card.

S

"SCRATCH": to erase or eradicate machine-readable information, either by accident or design.

SEQUENTIAL ACCESS DEVICE: a piece of computer hardware for the storage of data on which access to a particular address is such that the time required to transfer a unit of information to or from the storage is directly related to the location which is addressed (contrast with *direct access device*).

SETUP: a series of instructions, usually in the form of punch cards, which specify the parameters for control and operation of a computer program.

SNOBOL: a programming language designed for the manipulation of strings of characters and alphabetic text.

SOFTWARE: the set of programs and routines used to operate a computer.

SORT: to arrange the sequence or order of data records according to specified rules based upon the contents of designated data fields. The order is either ascending or descending in accord with the values of the sort fields.

SUBROUTINE: a set of instructions treated as a unit that performs a specific programming task.

SUBSET: a set contained within a set, usually referring to a selected portion of the variables and/or units of analysis in a dataset.

SYSTEM FILES: data files which have a predefined relationship to a particular technical format to facilitate fast and efficient data processing. They are created by and for the subsequent use of specific applications software packages.

T

TEST CODING: the process of developing a coding scheme by testing and refining a proposed set of code categories against a sample of the actual data. The information obtained by this process is used to adjust the code categories; when the test coding is completed, all of the data are then coded according to the final coding scheme.

TRACK: the path along which information is recorded on a storage device. On a magnetic tape this is equivalent to a channel consisting of a single row of serially recorded bits. On a disk, this is equivalent to a portion of a cylinder.

TSO: the interactive operating system distributed by IBM as its *T*ime *S*haring *O*ption.

TURNAROUND TIME: the elapsed time from the submission of a computer run to when the output is available.

U

UNIT OF ANALYSIS: the basic element of analysis, sometimes referred to as the case or observation, for which data are collected in the form of variables.

"UPDATING": the correction of a data record or the addition or replacement of data records in a data file.

V

VARIABLE: a quantity which can assume any of a set of values; a named data item in storage which may assume different values at different times during the running of a program.

VARIANCE: a statistical measure of the distribution of the values of a variable about the mean.

VERIFICATION: the process by which the original transcription of data to machine-readable form is checked for accuracy by replication of the data entry process. It is used as an error reduction technique as well as to establish the reliability of the transcription.

VERIFIER: a device used for the transcription of machine-readable data which checks the location of punches in cards by the simulation of the original punching.

VIRTUAL MEMORY: a conceptual form of main storage which does not really exist but is made to appear as if it did exist through the use of peripheral devices and programming. It results in the availability of memory space greater than the physical core storage of the computer.

Appendix

Sources of Information
About Available Computers and Software

It is impossible to enumerate completely all of the makes and models of computer hardware available from the numerous manufacturers or to list the full range of software and software services that are available. However, everyone interested in the use of computers and in assessing their applicability to specific tasks requires some central sources of information about available options in terms of capabilities, costs, and operation. There are two generally available sources of such information—a set of periodicals distributed without charge to a large number of interested individuals and reports from technical services which provide evaluative material for a fee on a wide range of computer equipment and services.

There are several widely distributed periodicals which are described as available to "qualified individuals" in computer-related positions or institutions. They have independent editorial staffs and are generally supported by advertising revenues. They often include mail surveys inserted in the magazine, and the analysis of reader responses often becomes copy for subsequent issues. Each of the publications is characterized by articles about administrative and management problems in the relevant area, and each has special departments devoted to reviews of new products and services in the data processing field. Most data processing personnel "subscribe" to one or more of these periodicals and would have copies available for inspection. For readers of this monograph who cannot find local copies we have included the publishers' addresses in the descriptions below:

Computer Decisions, a monthly publication of Hayden Publishing Co., Inc., 50 Essex Street, Rochelle Park, N.J. 07662. This magazine is "issued free of charge to qualified individuals with active professional and functional responsibility in computer manufacturing or the computer user industries." In addition to extensive advertisements with a high technical content, the magazine includes regular sections on "Systems," "Peripherals," and "Software."

Datamation, a monthly publication of Datamation Technical Publishing Company, 1301 South Grove Ave., Barrington, Illinois 60010. This magazine is "generally circulated without charge by name and title to certain qualified individuals in the United States and Canada who are employed by companies involved with automatic information handling equipment." The magazine includes regular departments on "Hardware" and "Software and Services."

Mini-Macro Systems, a monthly publication of Modern Data Services, 5 Kane Industrial Drive, Hudson, Massachusetts 01749. This magazine is distributed "free of charge to the business address of qualified individuals within the United States and Canada." The magazine has several departments relating to new products including "Data Entry," "Memories," "Components," "Terminals," "Systems," and "New Software."

SKINNY, a semiannual publication (April and October) of International Computer Programs, Inc., 1119 Keystone Way, Carmel, Indiana 46032. This publication is distributed free of charge as an abbreviated version of the *ICP Software Directory* which is published in January and July. The magazine is almost entirely composed of advertisements for proprietary software and software services, and it provides a general reference to the range of software options.

There are also a number of organizations which provide technical evaluations of available hardware and software. Generally these take the form of an annual subscription to the service which entitles the purchaser to a current volume of reports in loose-leaf form, to periodic updates, and new product information. These services are relatively expensive for individuals, but most computing centers maintain subscriptions to one or more. They provide an excellent reference in condensed form for individuals who are contemplating equipment purchases or conversions of equipment and are often used prior to inviting manufacturers or their representatives to supply more detailed information. The information includes technical specifications of equipment and current prices.

Auerbach Computer Technology Reports, a publication of Auerbach Publishers, Inc., Pennsauken, N.J. 08109. There are 11 major reports in the available series. Those of particular interest to readers would probably be "General Purpose Computer Systems," "Minicomputers," "Applications Software," and "Computer Terminals." Excerpts from the various technical reports are also published periodically in bound form.

DATAPRO Reports, a publication of Datapro Research Corporation, 1805 Underwood Boulevard, Delran, N.J. 08075. A standard in the field is *DATAPRO 70: The EDP Buyer's Bible,* which is a directory of 390 companies that offer products and services, especially hardware and software. Other publications include *Reports on Minicomputers* and a *Directory of Software.*

GML Minicomputer Review, a publication of GML Corporation, 594 Marrett Road, Lexington, Massachusetts 02173. As the name implies, these reports are directed to the increasing market for minicomputers and associated peripherals. The information is divided into separate sections for domestic and foreign manufacturers.

Composition by TypoGraphics, Columbia, Maryland